SUNSHINE STATE STRATEGY

SUNSHINE STATE STRATEGY

YOUR ESSENTIAL GUIDE TO
BECOMING A FLORIDA RESIDENT

RYAN KINSER & BRETT OLEY

Copyright © 2023 Ryan Kinser & Brett Oley
All rights reserved.

SUNSHINE STATE STRATEGY
Your Essential Guide to Becoming a Florida Resident

FIRST EDITION

ISBN   HARDCOVER: 978-1-5445-4239-3
       PAPERBACK: 978-1-5445-4237-9
       EBOOK: 978-1-5445-4238-6

RYAN KINSER:

To my beautiful wife, Dana, for being right by my side in all of our family and career endeavors. You, Kaia, Barron, Troy, and our growing family inspire me every day.

BRETT OLEY:

To my dearest Magnus and Langley—I love you beyond words! You are my everything. Love, Dad.

CONTENTS

Disclosure 9

INTRODUCTION	What's in It for You?	11
CHAPTER ONE	Why America's Most Successful People Are Moving to Florida	19
CHAPTER TWO	The Florida Resident Raise	33
CHAPTER THREE	Making Your House Your Home(stead)	45
CHAPTER FOUR	A Shield for Your Hard-Earned Assets	53
CHAPTER FIVE	Settling Down in the Sunshine State	61
CHAPTER SIX	Making Your Move	71
CHAPTER SEVEN	Estate Planning Essentials	79
CHAPTER EIGHT	Financially Planning as a Floridian	89
CHAPTER NINE	Building a Team to Win	99
CHAPTER TEN	Living and Thriving in Florida	105
CONCLUSION	Sunshine State Summary	111
APPENDIX	Additional Resources	115

About the Authors 119

DISCLOSURE

This book is educational in nature and not intended to cover every scenario. Please see the appropriate professionals for complete details on your situation. Any opinions are those of the authors and not necessarily those of Raymond James. There is no guarantee that these statements, opinions, or forecasts provided herein will prove to be correct. Any opinions are current as of the date of publication and subject to change. The information has been obtained from sources considered to be reliable, but Raymond James does not guarantee that the material is accurate or complete.

Any information is not a complete summary or statement of all available data necessary for making an investment decision and is not intended as a solicitation to buy or sell any security referred to herein nor does it constitute a recommendation. Investing involves risk and you may incur a profit or loss regardless of strategy selected. Graphs/charts are provided for illustrative purposes only.

The authors and Raymond James do not provide tax or legal services. Please discuss these matters with the appropriate professional. Raymond James is not affiliated with, and does not endorse, any individual, local, or state government/agency or any third party mobile application, such as TaxBird.

Certified Financial Planner Board of Standards Inc. owns the certification marks CFP®, CERTIFIED FINANCIAL PLANNER™, CFP® (with plaque design) and CFP® (with flame design) in the US, which it awards to individuals

DISCLOSURE

who successfully complete CFP Board's initial and ongoing certification requirements. CFA® and Chartered Financial Analyst® are registered trademarks owned by CFA Institute.

Authors Ryan Kinser and Brett Oley offer securities through Raymond James Financial Services, Inc., member FINRA/SIPC. Investment advisory services offered through Raymond James Financial Services Advisors, Inc. Oley Kinser Concierge Wealth is not a registered broker/dealer and is independent of Raymond James.

INTRODUCTION

WHAT'S IN IT FOR YOU?

PEOPLE ARE MOVING to Florida in record numbers! According to US Census Bureau data, Florida is now the number one destination for Americans seeking to relocate to a new state. While the trend has been going on for quite a while, it picked up steam in 2020. Indeed, from April 2020 to April 2021, almost 330,000 people became new residents of Florida. That's over 900 people a day! And it hasn't slowed down since then.

We see this firsthand practically every day. Retirees, business owners, corporate executives, affluent families, and investors come to us all the time asking how they can make the switch and establish a domicile here in Florida.

So what's driving all of these people to uproot from places they've known their whole lives to put down roots in the Sunshine State? Well, as it turns out, there are a few contributing factors. First, remote work has become far more common in recent years, due largely to a much more mobile economy, so more people now have the ability to take their job with them wherever they go. They're no longer tied to an office or stuck on a factory floor somewhere.

As long as they've got a laptop and a strong internet connection, they can work just about anywhere. That's given a whole lot of people the freedom to choose where they want to live outside of any career considerations, and many of them are looking for a home state that makes the most financial sense. And one thing that makes Florida especially attractive to working people is that it has no state income tax, which means many people get an instant pay raise the moment they establish residency in Florida.

Think about it. California currently has just over a 13 percent state income tax at the highest marginal rate, so when a California resident becomes a Florida resident, they potentially get to keep an extra 13 percent of their income! If you're a high earner, that could be a sizable amount of money.

Second, Florida has been, and continues to be, a popular retirement destination. The image of Florida being full of retirees is an old stereotype with a lot of truth to it, and it's been going on for decades. But why? Why do so many come here when their careers are over? At one time, it was probably driven primarily by the warm weather, but over time, more and more people are drawn here because Florida offers certain financial benefits for retirees (especially for people with a higher net worth and a sizable income).

Did you know there's currently no estate tax and no inheritance tax in Florida? In so many northern states (we'll talk about them later on), there's the potential for a large chunk of money to get taken out of an estate in taxes before the remainder is passed along to the heirs, so when retirees realize that Florida takes nothing, it provides a powerful incentive to relocate permanently. Additionally, Florida is very strong from a creditor perspective, so there are plenty of opportunities to protect all of the assets that you've worked hard to accumulate over the years.

Look, we live in a litigious and tax-hungry society, so anything you can do to protect your wealth and pass it on to your heirs can be incredibly attractive. Couple that with plenty of sunny days, warm weather, beaches, and world-famous tourist attractions, and the increasing appeal of Florida residency becomes clear.

MAKING FLORIDA YOUR HOME

The key to enjoying all of these financial benefits is becoming a Florida resident, and that means establishing a domicile. It might seem like this should be a simple thing. Just hire some movers and head south, right? But once people start digging into the process, it can quickly feel overwhelming. Particularly for the wealthy or those with a more complex picture.

There are just so many things you have to do, it's a bit like trying to climb a mountain. If you want to do it right, then you have to approach it from two different angles. First, there's the *quantitative* side to this, where you determine if it makes sense for you financially to make the move. Then, there's the *qualitative* side, where you have to figure out if it makes sense for you personally, and this is where so many people struggle. Becoming a Florida resident might make financial sense, but what about your kids and grandkids who live up north? Do you really want to spend most of the year down in Florida if it means missing out on time with loved ones? What about your friends up north and your further connections to business?

We spoke with a couple recently who were considering

moving from Illinois to Florida. Establishing a homestead down here makes perfect financial sense for them. It *slowly* caps any tax increases on their home, protects their assets, and allows them to keep more of their hard-earned income and estate. However, the emotional "costs" of moving away from their grandchildren proved to be too much. In the end, they decided to remain in Illinois for a few more years so they can spend time with the grandchildren as they grow up.

It's a big decision. It has to make sense financially *and* personally for you. There's a reason why so many people come and talk to us about becoming Florida residents. If there was no risk, it wouldn't be a big deal, but people have a lot of considerations and concerns. Beyond the financial and personal, they worry about being audited by their home state. Let's be honest, northern states can be quite aggressive when a wealthy family departs and takes away a source of revenue.

To steer clear of an audit or tax penalties, you have to make sure you do everything right and get your affairs in order. That way, you can sleep peacefully at night, confident that your former state's government isn't likely to come after you for committing the cardinal sin of taking your taxable income away from them. Florida will welcome you with open arms (that part is easy), but proving to your northern state that you have become a Floridian is what's so important. Your northern state is the "loser" in the equation since they're the ones losing revenue—thus making them more interested.

The good news is, you can become a Florida resident and enjoy all of those benefits without fear, doubt, or uncertainty. While it's never going to be as easy as flipping a switch, it doesn't have to be a grueling ordeal. Even so, it gets more complex the more wealth you have. For people with a lot of assets, it can sometimes take months to do it right, but we're

INTRODUCTION

going to help you check all the right boxes so you have peace of mind.

We wrote this book as an educational guide to walk you through the entire process of becoming a Florida resident *the right way*. When we work with clients, we lay it out as simply as possible so they can determine if the move makes sense for them, and then we walk them through the process step by step. That means providing the documentation they need to deliver to their local government center, sitting with them in estate planning meetings, and so much more.

Now, of course, we can't do all of that in a book, but what we can do is lay out the process in a streamlined, easy-to-read fashion so you can make your decision with confidence. Think of us as your Florida residency tour guides, giving you the lay of the land and pointing the way forward.

To be clear, while this book is a general guide that applies to most people, everyone's situation is unique. For that reason, we strongly encourage you to seek specific, customized guidance, especially if you have a high net worth. Think of this book as a primer that will help you get your bearings so you can start moving forward with your plans, but consider meeting with an expert one-on-one to deal with the nuances of your specific circumstances.

TWO ROADS TO FLORIDA

So, who are we, and why do we care so much about this subject? We're Ryan Kinser and Brett Oley, and we've helped hundreds of people make a successful transition from northern states to Florida. We've heard all of their stories, their concerns and worries, and we've helped them navigate their unique challenges. Along the way, we realized we could deliver the same advice to a lot more people through a book.

And as the number of people moving to Florida continues to increase, it's going to become more and more important to have a resource like this one.

Ryan has lived in Florida a majority of his life (aside from a few years in the Caribbean), and knows this state inside and out, but Brett came here from Ohio in 2006 so he has experienced becoming a Floridian firsthand. He understands the financial considerations and challenges in establishing Florida domicile and dealing with the scrutiny of a northern state.

Together, we've talked to hundreds of people about establishing Florida residency through the process individually. We've helped clients, friends, and even our own families to navigate this path. Ryan's father moved from Indiana to Florida many years ago. We're also financial advisors, so we focus on understanding a client and their needs *before* prescribing a solution. That means, in some cases, understanding the landscape and then helping them decide that it may not always be the right decision for them.

Watching this state continue to grow at such a rapid pace in the last couple of decades has been amazing. Consider the fact that a hundred years ago, the city where we live, Naples, was mostly a giant swamp, and today it's a thriving town full of nice homes and affluent people. When we drive around town, about a third of the license plates we see are from out of state.

There are so many good reasons why this is happening. Yes, we have to endure hurricane season, and that's not fun. Summer's a bit humid, but it's not as hot as some people would have you believe. You can have a good life in Florida. You can protect your assets, protect your home, and have peace of mind that your future is secure for your heirs.

If it's right for you, we want to help you make that journey,

INTRODUCTION

and that's exactly what this book is meant to do. Use this as a reference to guide you as you consider, decide, and then make the move. We'll help you weigh the pros and cons, so you can make an educated decision. Even if you're just considering the possibility and "doing your homework," with no intention to move down here anytime soon, this book can at least provide some food for thought. Knowledge is power, and we want you to be armed!

Or, maybe your decision to move is imminent, in which case this book will prove to be an invaluable source of information for the days ahead. Of course, if you need one-on-one advice, feel free to contact us directly, and we'll give you personalized guidance through every step of the process; this book's purpose is to give you all of the basic information you need.

Bear in mind, we can't provide specific tax or legal advice in a book like this. For that, you need to meet with your CPA or an estate planning attorney—and meeting with these professionals throughout the process is highly encouraged as well. However, you should come away with a good idea of the overall process for establishing a Florida domicile, as well as the many benefits you can take advantage of. You'll understand some of the potholes in the road that you need to avoid, so you can make the move successfully. And if you decide to become a Florida resident, we want to be the first to welcome you to the great Sunshine State!

But first, let's understand what's really going on in the US that is driving so many people to pack up and head south.

CHAPTER ONE

WHY AMERICA'S MOST SUCCESSFUL PEOPLE ARE MOVING TO FLORIDA

THE CONTINUED INFLUX of high-net-worth individuals to Florida has gathered steam in recent years. We've personally seen numerous families making the move. We've also seen corporations relocating to the state: hedge funds, private equity firms, investment firms, manufacturing companies, service-based enterprises, and other companies all making the move to Florida. And all of those owners and their employees may receive new-found tax breaks. The vast majority of the people we meet with on the topic of Florida domicile are from a variety of industries and backgrounds—generally, most are self-made or entrepreneurial business owners—but all share the common drive to keep more of their hard-earned money.

CHAPTER ONE

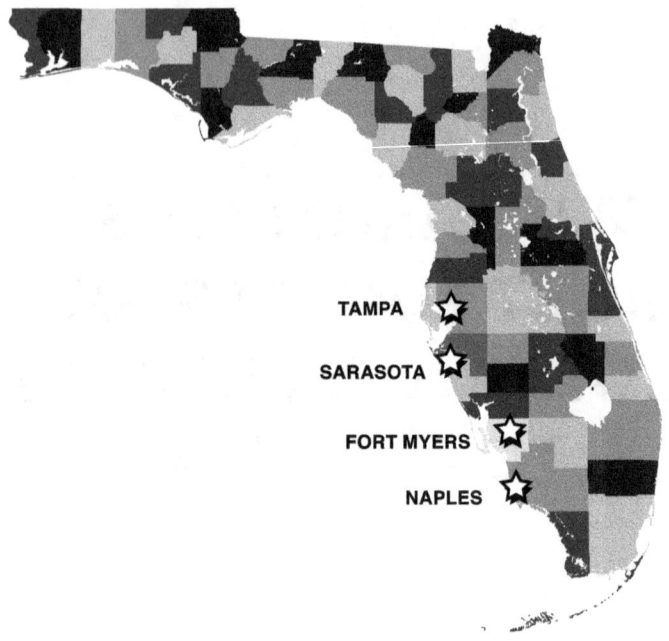

On a list of the twenty-five fastest growing cities in the United States published in *U.S. News & World Report* in early 2023, *eleven* of them were located in Florida—almost half of the entire list! This includes popular destinations like Naples, Sarasota, Fort Myers, and Tampa.[1]

So Florida's economy, tax situation, climate, and culture are clearly very attractive to people from northern states. In particular, many are drawn here by the lack of a state income

---

[1] Devon Thorsby, "The 25 Fastest-Growing Places in the U.S.," Real Estate, U.S. News, March 30, 2023, https://realestate.usnews.com/real-estate/slideshows/the-fastest-growing-places-in-the-us.

tax. If you come from highly taxed states like California, New York, or Minnesota, that means you potentially get an instant pay raise by becoming a Florida resident. That one benefit alone is enough for many people, especially those with a higher income, to convince them to make the move.

The fact that thousands of successful people are moving to Florida every year from all across the United States should raise an eyebrow. Haven't you wondered what all of these people know that you don't know? We've already shared with you a few of the financial benefits that are bringing them here, but there's so much more.

If you've been financially successful, you probably spend quite a bit of time trying to figure out how you can keep what you've worked so hard to acquire, or how you can protect it after you're gone so it can be passed along to your loved ones, rather than the government. Clearly, you've done quite a few things right to get to this point. You've been smart and savvy about your investments and income, but how can you continue to protect the fruits of your labor and all your discipline and sacrifices?

All of those intelligent decisions won't do you much good if you can't protect your assets. Well, Florida provides some unique protections that can enable you to keep more of your own money, and the state offers robust creditor protections. No wonder successful people are moving here in droves!

WHAT DO THEY KNOW?

Chances are, some of your own friends, relatives, and peers have made the move. They've come here from many places like New York, New Jersey, Ohio, Minnesota, Pennsylvania, Michigan, and Indiana, among others! You've perhaps watched this happening from afar, and it has piqued your interest.

CHAPTER ONE

"Florida must be a nice place," you've thought. "My friends and family seem to be really happy down there. Maybe I should look into this."

And maybe this book is part of your effort to investigate the possibility. Well, you've come to the right place, but if you've noticed, this isn't a pamphlet or a one-page flyer. Clearly, there's a lot more to say on this subject than, "People move here because there's no state income tax."

As it turns out, there are a lot more benefits to living in Florida, and a lot more many more steps involved in the process of establishing residency in such a way that it protects your assets and allows you to enjoy all of the benefits.

Now, you might think that moving to Florida requires a big trade-off. Yes, you get some financial benefits, but on the other hand, you have to live in a hot, muggy, boring state full of sleepy retirees who play checkers all day. That was perhaps at one time the perception of Naples, the city where we live and work. But we're here to tell you that if that's your view of Florida, then you're respectfully behind the times. Speaking for our community, this is a vibrant place with a lot of active people enjoying their lives. They play golf and tennis, take walks on the beach, go boating, and participate in plenty of other cultural and leisure activities.

Yes, it's warm down here, but in all honesty, it's not too hot for most of the year. There's rain, but there are also plenty of sunny days (on average, 264 sunny days per year here in Naples).[2] And there's so much to see and do that it could keep you busy for the rest of your life. We say this not only from our own personal experience; we've also seen it in the lives of

---

2 "Naples, Florida," Best Places, accessed April 6, 2023, https://www.bestplaces.net/climate/city/florida/naples.

the hundreds of clients we've worked with. They're not just protecting their assets and keeping more of their own money by living in Florida, they are also having the time of their lives!

And Florida is a very diverse state. You can find a region and city that perfectly matches your personality and preferences. In fact, we'll give you a cultural overview of the entire state at the end of this book, so stay tuned.

The point is, you benefit from more than just a few tax quirks. You can also live a better, happier, and more exciting life in Florida, which could help you live longer. There are far more opportunities to get outside, stay active, and create a social life, and with the sun shining most of the year, you'll get plenty of vitamin D.

A longer, happier life where you get to keep more of your money, protect your assets, and pass along more to your heirs? That sounds like a pretty good deal, doesn't it?

So who, exactly, is moving to Florida? According to a recent study, the states that are sending the most people to Florida are New York, Pennsylvania, Ohio, California, New Jersey, Virginia, Illinois, Michigan, Indiana, Massachusetts, Pennsylvania, and Maryland.[3] Not surprisingly, many of these states, with a few notable exceptions, have the reputation for being high-tax states.

Some states are even seeing a decline in overall population (e.g., New York at -1.58%, Illinois at -0.89%. and California at -0.66%), as more people are leaving than entering.[4] We've

---

3 "States Sending the Most People to Florida," Stacker, July 10, 2022, https://stacker.com/florida/states-sending-most-people-florida.
4 "States Losing Population 2023," World Population Review, 2023, https://worldpopulationreview.com/state-rankings/states-losing-population.

met some of these people. They shake their heads at what's happening economically, culturally, or politically in their old home state and say things like, "I'm so glad we made the move to Florida. Our old state isn't what it once was. We're doing so much better here!"

A STATE IN GOOD SHAPE

Let's look a little closer at some of the big benefits you can acquire by establishing residency in Florida. Since these are the major draw for so many successful people who are moving here (and there's a good chance they are the primary reason you're reading this book), we want to make sure you have a full understanding of what's available to you here.

We've mentioned a few benefits already, but let's look at them in a bit more depth. First, Florida is a relatively low-tax environment, which is particularly beneficial to people with a high income. The state government tends to be extremely fiscally responsible with the state budget and, relative to revenue, keeps spending low, so economically Florida is in very strong shape. A direct effect of this fiscal approach is that taxes have also remained relatively low, and the state has never implemented an income tax.

They don't need the money from income taxes because the government tends to set a very conservative budget. In fact, in the year we wrote this book, the state had a massive revenue surplus.

With a conservative budget, Florida's government isn't money hungry, so there's no clamoring for more. How, then, does the state fund its budget? As it turns out, Florida largely lives and breathes off its sales tax, which is nice because it's entirely a discretionary expense. In other words, you control how much sales tax you pay simply by regulating your purchases along the way. When you buy something, you pay the sales tax right then and there, unlike income tax, which takes a cut of the money you've already earned right off the top.

Additionally, much of the sales tax is driven by the theme parks, hotels, merchants, tourist attractions, and all of the other activities taking place across the state, which means tourists and visitors are constantly dumping a huge amount of money into the government's coffers. That softens the impact on taxpayers, but it also encourages lawmakers to create and maintain a business-friendly environment. Florida has one of the lowest corporate tax rates in the country (the second lowest in the nation, as of this writing, and most small businesses pay no corporate taxes at all).[5] Plus, companies have a lot of freedom and flexibility here.

We saw the impact of this attitude firsthand during the dark days of 2020. Other state governments were shutting down businesses all over the place and in all kinds of industries, whereas Florida took a wildly different approach. Florida gave business owners the freedom to do what they thought was best when it came to things like business continuity. As a result, many businesses and their workers flourished here.

Our own financial wealth advisory practice benefited tremendously from the freedom Florida provided because we were able to stay open and find ways to continue to serve our clients well across the state and country. In Florida, we watched from afar as restaurants, nightclubs, shops, and

---

5 Greg Depersio, "Taxes in Florida for Small Businesses: The Basics," Investopedia, last updated January 31, 2021, https://www.investopedia.com/articles/personal-finance/101315/taxes-florida-small-businesses-basics.asp.

CHAPTER ONE

thousands of small businesses in places like New York and California were driven into the ground.

Indeed, some of the owners of those businesses have since made the move down here. Imagine being a restaurateur in New York City, trying to get by with just a few customers restricted to a few tables on the sidewalk, and watching your business slowly fading away. Then you go online and see restaurants and bars in Florida that are open and jam-packed with customers and full of reservations. No wonder so many of them have made the move! In that case, moving to Florida became more than just a plan to gain some financial advantage. It was a decision driven by the will to survive!

We point this out because it was fully in line with Florida's business-friendly environment with minimal regulations, which is as true now as it was then. Indeed, the business relocation boom that began in 2020 has continued full steam to this day.[6]

Another important benefit of being a Florida resident is homestead asset protection, which is written into the state constitution. We'll look at this benefit a bit more later, but in essence, it ensures that your primary residence (you can have only one, and in this case we're speaking of Florida) can't be taken away from you and has impediments on increased taxation.

Beyond financial benefits, there are the benefits of coastal living. Most places in Florida are within easy driving distance

---

6   David Lyons, "As COVID Rolled On, Legions of Companies Migrated to Florida. Which Metro Areas Gained the Most?" *South Florida Sun-Sentinel*, May 15, 2022, https://www.sun-sentinel.com/business/fl-bz-florida-company-relocations-20220515-pygta6tmorcuvcrlq522xu5tva-story.html.

of the beach and often within walking distance. There are plenty of affluent neighborhoods built right along the state's many, many beaches, and so much of the year is warm that you can enjoy the beach or the state's many parks in every season.

THE DOWNSIDE OF LIVING IN FLORIDA

Florida has a beautiful climate if you love sunshine and warm weather. As we like to tell people from other states, "We live where you vacation." But, look, living in Florida *does* have some downsides. Yes, hurricanes are a real thing that Floridians have to deal with. We can go many years with no hurricanes, but when they have a direct hit, they can be a big problem.

Additionally, the heat may be too much for some people. If you've ever visited the theme parks in Orlando with your family on summer vacation, you know exactly what we're talking about! In fact, fifty years ago, before air conditioning was common, the heat and humidity in Florida were truly miserable for about half the year, and you couldn't really go anywhere to escape the misery.

Of course, that's rarely a problem now, because private homes and public facilities are almost always air conditioned. Air conditioning first became common in Florida in the middle of the 1960s, and the population began to grow dramatically shortly after that.[7] This probably isn't a coincidence. I don't

---

7   Jeff Kunerth, "In Florida, Life without Air Conditioning Can Be Suffocating," *Orlando Sentinel*, September 4, 2013, https://www.orlandosentinel.com/features/os-florida-without-air-conditioning-20130904-story.html.

think either of us would live here if we couldn't escape the heat. As a history professor at the University of South Florida put it, "Florida as we know it would not exist without air conditioning."

Even when it's not blazingly hot, in many parts of Florida, it rains at least a little bit almost every day during the summer (our "rainy season"), so that might take some getting used to—but it does cool things off! The point is, Florida isn't a perfect paradise, and we're not making the claim that you won't have any problems or inconveniences if you move here. You have to decide if the move makes sense for you.

From a financial perspective, in our experience, one of the only things Florida scrutinizes is whether or not you're trying to use state tax benefits to protect your home up north. If you have homes in both Florida *and* your former state, you will need to talk to a CPA to make sure you are using the homestead exemption properly. If you have a nice home up north somewhere, you're likely to have to terminate your homestead exemption in order to move it to Florida. In short, you can maintain only one homestead.

Keep in mind, forfeiting or terminating your northern homestead exemption (you can still keep the house), particularly in those states with a material homestead exemption, can result in greater taxes on that northern home. We have found this to be the case particularly in Indiana and Michigan, which carry substantive homestead tax benefits. It is also important to note that this is one potential disadvantage, and it may be greatly outweighed by other positive benefits and factors.

Now, if you have some sentimental attachment to your northern home, or a lot invested in it, this can be a difficult decision and a significant loss. It's not an uncommon dilemma. Many high-net-worth Florida residents have homes in multiple states. Often, when they move here, they keep their home up north. But let's suppose you have a large gain on your northern property, and it's now worth a lot more than it was when you bought it. Add on to this that you also have the intention to sell that property—is that going to be a problem?

If you ever intend to sell the northern house, you're going to have to do it within three years of moving to Florida to take advantage of a taxable exclusion. Currently the IRS allows you to exclude up to $250,000 of the capital gain on that property (or $500,000 if you file jointly) but only if it's been your primary residence.[8] To be more precise, if you've used the house in two out of the last five years as your primary residence, then the clock starts ticking, so from the time you move to Florida (and establish a new primary residence), you have three years to sell your northern home or you'll lose the exclusion. And what happens then? All of that gain on the home's value becomes taxable!

Beyond these downsides, there are the intangible side effects of leaving your northern state that are unique to your situation. Will you have to leave loved ones behind? Will you be moving away from friends, children, grandchildren, or other relatives? Can you still run your business as well as you've done in the past by working remotely? Just because someone moves from New York to Florida doesn't mean they were tired of New York. In fact, some of the people who move here for financial reasons find it difficult or painful to leave a place they loved and that was such a big part of their lives.

---

[8] "Topic No. 701 Sale of Your Home," IRS, last updated January 27, 2023, https://www.irs.gov/taxtopics/tc701.

CHAPTER ONE

BOTH SIDES OF THE COIN

As you can see, there are a lot of different aspects to this decision. How can you decide if moving to Florida is the right choice for you? Just remember, you have to consider this from two sides: your current state and your future state. There's the good you hope to gain, and the pressure you hope to escape.

Let's suppose you're currently located in northern Ohio, and you're considering moving to Florida. On one side of the coin, there's plenty of warm weather down here. On the other side of the coin, there are the harsh gray winters up north. You want to enjoy plenty of sunny days, but you also want to escape the Seasonal Affective Disorder caused by six months of overcast cold weather!

You have to look at it from both sides to truly weigh if it's worth the hard work to leave your current home and establish residency in Florida. You may ask, "What is pushing me away from my northern state, and what is pulling me to Florida?" It's a very different lifestyle down here, after all. From the climate, to lower taxes, to greater freedom, there are many good reasons why people of all ages are coming to Florida. You don't have to be a retiree to make a much better life for yourself here.

Do you like boating and fishing? Florida has some of the best fishing in the country. Do you prefer sports and fitness? Maybe you love the beach. We have beaches in nearly every part of the state. Beyond that, there's a lot of diversity across Florida. If you like the big city, you can move to Miami, Orlando, or Tampa. If you want to live off the grid, there are plenty of tiny towns tucked away in the woods and swamps. There's northern Florida, which has a vibe like the

Deep South. There are the Florida Keys, which offer a relaxed island vibe.

You can see why so many people are being drawn here. Now, it's time to weigh your own decision. Look at both sides of the coin—what you'll be leaving, and what you'll be gaining—and consider your options. You might conclude that it's time to get your act in gear. You might think, "I've done a lot in my career. I've been successful. I need to move somewhere that will make it easier to protect my assets, live a better life, and protect my financial legacy, and I need to do it soon!"

Maybe it's time to sit down with a piece of paper and draw up your pros and cons, so you can make an informed decision. Before you do that, let us clarify the financial reality of moving to Florida so you can gain a clearer sense of how it will impact you to make the change.

CHAPTER TWO

THE FLORIDA RESIDENT RAISE

AN INSTANT PAY raise sounds pretty good, doesn't it? That's what you might get when you move to a state with no income tax. If you move from New York to Florida, you'll likely get to keep a good portion of your income that formerly went to state income tax (based on the highest tax bracket). If you come from Minnesota or California, you're likely in a very similar scenario. Even if you come from a state that has low state income tax, you can still enjoy an instant pay raise, and that's always a nice thing. Ohio's highest state income tax bracket is currently 3.99 percent, but if you have a high income, that's still a large chunk of change that you potentially get to keep by moving to Florida.[9]

---

[9] Timothy Vermeer, "State Individual Income Tax Rates and Brackets for 2023," Tax Foundation, February 21, 2023, https://taxfoundation.org/publications/state-individual-income-tax-rates-and-brackets/.

But here's the thing: even if you don't get paid by an employer, you can still get a pay raise just by becoming a Florida resident. Chances are you've saved some money in a qualified retirement account, such as an IRA or 401(k). Well, at a certain age, you're required by the government to take money out of that account. The age at which these required minimum distributions take place tends to change according to the whims of Congress.

Most of the time, these required distributions are considered ordinary income, and they're taxed at among the highest rate. If you're in a high-tax state that applies their state income tax to retirement account distributions, then they're going to take a big piece of your retirement income from required distributions.

By moving to Florida, you might no longer have to worry about paying any state income tax on your retirement account distributions. So even if you're retired and no longer working, you can still enjoy an instant pay raise. More of your own money in your pocket. That's never a bad thing.

So many of the future Floridians who come to us want to know how the markets are performing. They want to know their rate of return on their investments and the relative risk that they are taking, because they're focused on saving and growing their wealth. But here's a way to keep an extra portion of your own income in your own pocket instantly, all things being equal! That sounds like a really good investment to us.

It's not just about keeping more of your money for yourself. It's also about preserving more of your money for your estate so you can pass it along to your loved ones. If you own a home in Minnesota and you pass away there, your heirs could potentially have to pay an estate tax of 13 to 16 percent on the value of your home if your estate is worth more than $3 million.[10] Currently, eighteen states have either estate taxes or inheritance taxes, with Hawaii and Washington being the highest.[11]

However, Florida has neither an estate tax *nor* an inheritance tax. The state government probably isn't going to take a dime of what you have worked so hard to build and eventually leave behind. The state will not confiscate a portion from your heirs, so your legacy is protected from a state estate tax perspective. Of course, you'll want to keep in mind a potential estate tax at the federal level. In a state like Minnesota, 16 percent of the estate of a high-net-worth individual can easily mean millions and millions of dollars getting siphoned away from their loved ones by the state government. For most everyone, this is the last beneficiary that they wish to name. The fact that becoming a Florida resident can instantly preserve millions of dollars of your estate makes the state incredibly attractive to people with a high net worth.

After all, why should the state get so much of what you've worked so hard to build? Why shouldn't you be able to leave that money for the people you choose? Now, to be clear, it requires some proactive estate planning to take full advantage of this benefit, especially if you move from a state with estate taxes, but the advantages of doing so are clear.

---

10   "Estate Tax Rates," Minnesota Department of Revenue, accessed April 6, 2023, https://www.revenue.state.mn.us/estate-tax-rates.
11   "18 States with Scary Death Taxes," Kiplinger, accessed April 6, 2023, https://www.kiplinger.com/retirement/inheritance/601551/states-with-scary-death-taxes.

CHAPTER TWO

IS IT TOO GOOD TO BE TRUE?

Maybe all of this sounds too good to be true. For some people, maybe you're thinking, "I get to keep millions and millions of dollars just by moving to Florida? What's the catch? There has to be some trick to it. Otherwise, *everyone* would move to Florida."

So we'll level with you. Yes, you have to be careful navigating this path, because there's always the risk of an audit, especially from the state you leave behind. In our experience, the size of that risk depends on how big of a fish you are. States don't like to lose high-net-worth residents, and if you take your millions out of state, there's a chance they could try to take a last bite out of your assets on the way out. In our opinion, the states that seem most likely to audit people on their way out are New York, New Jersey, Connecticut, Massachusetts, Illinois, Pennsylvania, and Minnesota, in no particular order.

They could ask you to prove you're a Floridian before they concede that they've lost you. Florida isn't the problem. You will be welcomed here with open arms. You don't have to prove much of anything to Florida. It's the northern state you leave behind that must be appeased because, from their perspective, you're taking money out of their coffers. They are the curious ones. They're going to want you to prove that you are, in fact, actually a resident of Florida, not just putting on the appearance of changing state residency in order to protect your income and assets from high state taxes.

Think of it from a business perspective. If your former state is considering dedicating resources and personnel to potentially auditing you, they most likely expect to recoup more in revenue than they are spending. If you're an average retiree leaving Illinois, the state might only lose about $10,000 a year in income taxes. That's not likely enough to justify investing in the resources to audit you.

But if you have a high net worth and the state stands to lose $500,000 a year or more, then you're likely to be of high interest and the risks for you certainly go up. And there's a good chance they're going to audit you to make sure it's all above board. Logically, a state government isn't going to let $500,000 a year in tax dollars (in just one year—imagine the lost future cash flows) easily slip through their fingers without considering some way to stop it from happening.

Even if you're as clean as a whistle, if you do everything right, they are almost sure to scrutinize your change of residency. Their thinking is simple: "Hey, $500,000 a year is $5 million over a decade. We need that money in Illinois' economy! We need it for our state budget!"

As we said, some states are a lot more aggressive about this than others. If you're from one of those states, you'll want to make sure all the more that you do everything right and have a paper trail to prove your residency. Moreover, if you have been paying higher state income tax revenues in the past to that northern state, in some cases, regardless of the state, then your risks can increase.

Now, there are some special circumstances we've come across, particularly in relation to business owners, that introduce some additional complexity. For example, if a lot of your taxable income comes from a K-1 income distribution rather than a W2, then certain northern states could continue to recognize it as income from your former state and there isn't much you can do about it.

If you receive revenue from a rental property that is physically located in certain northern states, then it becomes a lot harder to make the case that you shouldn't pay income tax in those states. Even so, we recommend working with a CPA or estate planning attorney who can provide specific advice for individual states.

Ultimately, in our opinion, there are two things that seem to increase your likelihood of getting audited: how big of a fish you are, and how big the state's financial need is. This isn't so much a "trick" as it is something you need to be aware of. If you're moving out of a high-tax state, you need to be more careful about doing everything the right way so you can protect yourself from a resentful "losing" state.

COULD IT ALL GO AWAY?

But what if all of these benefits we're talking about suddenly went away? What if you go through the entire process of moving to Florida, finally get settled, and then the state decides to implement a state income tax? Is it possible?

This is a fair question. Could the state of Florida decide to implement a state income tax, or an estate or inheritance tax, at some point in the future? Technically, yes, they *could* do it. It's within their power, but we believe it's *highly, highly* unlikely. First of all, implementing such a change would take a strong majority of the state legislature, and it wouldn't have widespread voter support.

More than that, the state of Florida is well aware of the fact that instituting a state income tax could immediately stem the tide of people coming here. The influx of new residents, especially high-net-worth individuals, would likely come to a screeching halt, and no elected official wants to be responsible for killing the growth of their state. Any benefit in increased tax revenue would be offset by the loss of revenue from a growing affluent population. Moreover, millions of people already live here, and they are enjoying said financial benefits. How many of them would then depart for another state with no state income taxes?

Historically, especially in recent decades, Florida has operated with a conservative budget, which has led to a budget surplus in recent years (a whopping $21.8 billion surplus in fiscal year 2021 to 2022).[12] There's no compelling reason to change this. Additionally, as more affluent people come into the state, there are going to be more and more voters with a vested interest in preserving the state's financially friendly climate.

Remember, Florida is fiscally very strong, a triple-A-rated ("AAA") state.[13] All three of the major credit rating agencies in the financial world—Moody's, Standard & Poor's, and Fitch—have given Florida a triple-A rating. There's only a handful of states that rate so highly. There's just no compelling reason to implement a state income tax.

For all of these reasons, we believe you can have confidence and peace of mind that the situation isn't going to change, not in our lifetimes.

And what about estate taxes, inheritance taxes, or gift taxes? Is it likely that Florida will implement anything like this in the future? As you may know, in many states, if you give your heirs too much money either in a given year or throughout your lifetime, they have to pay tax on it. Often,

---

12 "Governor Ron DeSantis Announces Record Surplus for Fiscal Year 2021–22," news release, July 7, 2022, Florida.gov, https://www.flgov.com/2022/07/07/governor-ron-desantis-announces-record-surplus-for-fiscal-year-2021-22/.
13 "S&P Announces Florida's AAA Credit Rating Ranks Higher than the Nation," news release, November 12, 2021, Florida.gov, https://www.flgov.com/2021/11/12/sp-announces-floridas-aaa-credit-rating-ranks-higher-than-the-nation/.

this is a one-two punch, because there's both a federal tax component and a state tax component. However, in Florida, there is no estate tax, gift tax, or inheritance tax at the state level, even for people of a very high net worth.

You may still have to contend with the federal estate tax, but eliminating the state component can make a huge difference. This is unlikely to change for the very same reasons that Florida is unlikely to ever implement a state income tax.

WHAT ABOUT PROPERTY TAXES?

Of course, income taxes, estate taxes, and inheritance taxes are not the only kinds of taxes that a high-net-worth individual has to worry about. There are also property taxes, and in Florida these vary by county. As you can see in the chart below, Florida fares well compared to a number of other states in this regard. For example, they are lower here than in Texas (an average of 0.97 percent versus an average rate of 1.81 percent).[14]

---

14 Victoria Araj, "Property Taxes by State: A Comparative Look at the Highest to Lowest States," Rocket Mortgage, February 14, 2023, https://www.rocketmortgage.com/learn/property-taxes-by-state.

MEDIAN PROPERTY TAX RATES BY STATE[15]

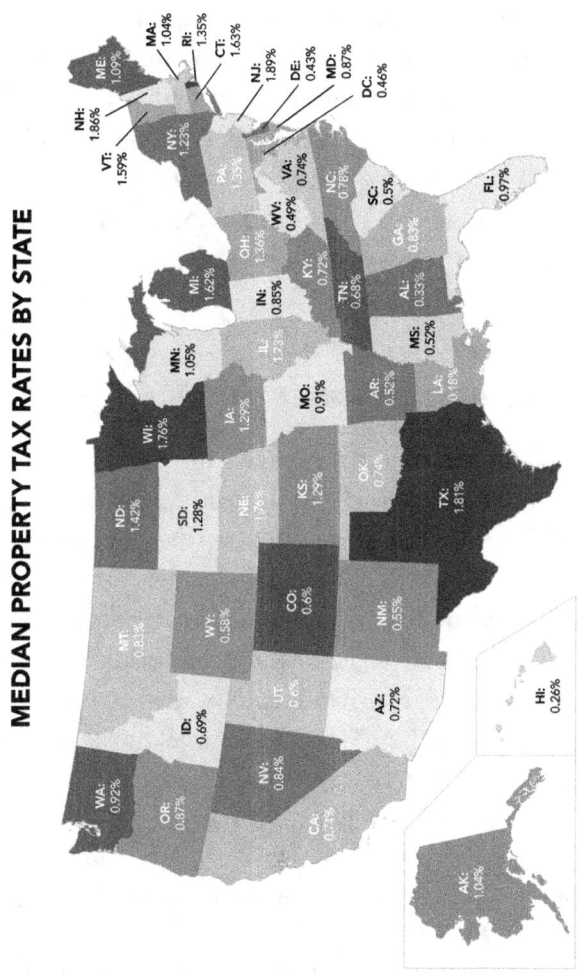

"Property Taxes by State," Tax-Rates.org, accessed April 6, 2023, http://www.tax-rates.org/taxtables/property-tax-by-state.

---

15   "Property Taxes by State," Tax-Rates.org, accessed April 6, 2023, http://www.tax-rates.org/taxtables/property-tax-by-state.

It's important to remember that property taxes in Florida are a key driver of the school systems across the state. Where we live, in Collier County, for example, a material portion of property tax revenue goes to support public schools. This, in turn, has created a robust educational system in Florida, which makes it more attractive to younger families. After all, nobody wants to live in an area with terrible, underperforming schools, so even if Florida doesn't have the lowest property taxes in the country, we consider it a reasonable trade-off.

SO, HOW DO THEY MAKE MONEY?

No estate tax, no inheritance tax, no gift tax, no income tax—so how in the world does Florida make money to run the state? How are they so fiscally strong, and how can they possibly have a surplus? Well, as we mentioned earlier, the state makes a whole lot of money from sales tax.

Florida has been a tourist destination for decades, but even in the last few years, tourism has exploded like never before. People are coming here for the theme parks in Orlando. They're coming here to relax on the East Coast beaches. They're coming here to have a wild weekend in Miami, or to go boating in the Gulf, on the Atlantic, or even on our many lakes. They come here to go fishing, to camp, to shop, and to enjoy themselves.

Approximately 137.6 million people visit Florida every year, and they come here from all over the world.[16] No matter

---

16 "Research FAQ," Visit Florida, accessed April 6, 2023, https://www.visitflorida.org/resources/research/research-faq/.

what their individual pursuits or interests, all tourists do one thing: *they spend money*. They spend a lot of money!

It's fair to say Florida lives and dies by the sword when it comes to sales tax. When we say tourists spend a lot of money, we're not exaggerating. Here in Naples, you can often rent a room at the Ritz Carlton for anywhere between $1,000 and $2,000 a night in the seasonal part of the year (January to April). That might sound like a crazy amount of money for a hotel room, but the hotel is regularly filled to capacity. Demand is through the roof!

Every time a tourist rents a room at the Ritz Carlton, roughly 7 percent of the money goes to sales tax. That's $70 to $140 going into the state's coffers every time someone rents a room at the Ritz Carlton in Naples, and the hotel has 447 guest rooms, thirty-five suites, and seventy club-level rooms. Do the math. That's a lot of sales tax, and that's just a single hotel in a single city!

Think about all of the hotels and resorts throughout Naples and across Southwest Florida. Then think about all of the hotels across the entire state. And that doesn't take into account all of the tourist tchotchkes, the meals, the park tickets, clothing, and everything else tourists and residents are buying every single day all year long.

As you can see, sales tax generates a massive amount of revenue for the state, especially during tourist seasons when the weather is great. So, quite frankly, Florida doesn't *need* state income tax (or many of the other types of tax) revenue.

MORE BANG FOR YOUR BUCK

Ultimately, the higher your net worth and the more income you generate per year, then the more bang for your buck you're likely going to get from the tax benefits of moving to Florida.

Indeed, the creditor protection elements of Florida, including the homestead provision in the state constitution, can protect both you and your family if something bad happens. Still, even with all of these benefits, you have to be willing to uproot your family from a state where you may have deep roots. Maybe you've lived there your entire life.

Maybe you were born and raised in Indiana, and you're a Hoosier to the core. Are you really ready to step away from all of that? Even if you keep some kind of home in your northern state, you're going to have to live primarily in Florida. That's a big change.

The good news is, Florida has everything you could want. And once you set up a residence in Florida, your primary residence here can be protected by the state's homestead exemption in a way that simply isn't available in many northern states.

Let's take a look at that homestead exemption next.

CHAPTER THREE

MAKING YOUR HOUSE YOUR HOME(STEAD)

THE LACK OF state income tax is, without question, the main driver that brings so many people to Florida. However, there is another benefit that is just as important, though it's far less known. In fact, many of the people we talk to haven't even heard about it until we tell them, despite the fact that it's one of the best benefits of its kind in the country.

What is this amazing benefit? Actually, it's two things that are related: Florida's homestead exemption and the "Save Our Homes" amendment to the state constitution.[17] Let's look at each of them.

"Save Our Homes" was a 1995 amendment to the Florida state constitution that limits the annual increase in

---

17 "Save Our Homes Assessment Limitation and Portability Transfer," Florida Department of Revenue, accessed April 6, 2023, https://floridarevenue.com/property/Documents/pt112.pdf.

the assessed value of your primary residence to 3 percent or the change in the National Consumer Price Index (CPI), whichever is less. The homestead exemption is a property tax break that reduces the assessed value of your home by as much as $50,000.[18] You qualify for the homestead exemption as soon as you establish residency in Florida, which could mean you get over $500 in tax savings right away (and up to every year thereafter as you qualify).

*Measured by the Consumer Price Index (CPI)
https://www.bls.gov/cpi

"Save Our Homes Assessment Limitation and Portability Transfer," Florida Department of Revenue, accessed April 6, 2023, https://floridarevenue.com/property/Documents/pt112.pdf; "Non-Homestead Cap (10%)," Miami-Date Property Appraiser, accessed April 27, 2023, https://www.miamidade.gov/pa/property_value_cap.asp.

The exemption can only be applied to your primary residence, and each individual can only have one. So, even if you own multiple residences and you move back and forth between them, the exemption can only be applied to one.

---

18   See Article VII, Section 6, of the Florida Constitution: https://www.flsenate.gov/Laws/Constitution#A7S06.

Also, since this is considered your residence, it can't be a regular rental property. To qualify, the following must be true:
- You own the property.
- The property is your permanent residence and the residence of your dependents.
- You've lived in the property since January 1 of the current tax year.
- The property hasn't been rented for more than thirty days of the current calendar year.

PROTECTING YOUR HOME

Once you've established a primary residence in Florida, and you've collected all of the appropriate paperwork to prove it (we'll talk about those documents later), then you can file for the Florida Homestead Exemption. Doing this provides you with a number of distinct benefits.

First, it protects your primary residence from creditors. Of course, there are always exceptions to this rule, and there are a few situations in which creditors can still touch the value of the home, but even then, the amount is greatly limited. Think about it. You could own a $20 million beachfront mansion and the homestead exemption may protect it from creditors!

Second, as we already mentioned, the "Save Our Homes" amendment caps the annual increase in the assessed value of your home at the lesser of either 3 percent or the Consumer Price Index (CPI), so even as real estate property values rise, you have the peace of mind of knowing that your own property taxes won't go through the roof as well. This is especially helpful because real estate in Florida has appreciated materially in the last two years with the influx of all the new people.

It's a benefit that compounds over time and becomes stronger as the cap applies to your home year after year. If you're *not* homesteaded in Florida but you own a home here, your property value increase is capped at 10 percent. We've seen situations where someone who has been homesteaded in Florida for many years (and enjoyed the cumulative effects of the homestead cap over a long period of time) is living beside someone who has been in Florida just as long, but not yet filed for homestead. They live in similar homes, and they've lived there for a similar period of time, but they pay *dramatically* different amounts of property taxes. Homestead is a long game that is in a Florida resident's favor.

Additionally, as we said, there's an immediate exemption that is applied to the first $50,000 of your property's assessed value if your property is your permanent residence and you owned the property on January 1 of the current tax year. This exemption applies to all taxes, including school district taxes. Here is how it works:

- Up to $25,000 in value is exempted from the first $50,000 in assessed value of your primary residence.
- You pay the full taxes on any value between $25,000 and $50,000.
- For any assessed value between $50,000 and $75,000, an additional $25,000 is also eligible for exemption.
- Properties valued at more than $75,000 are exempt at the previous levels, but then fully taxed for the portion over $75,000.[19]

---

19 "Property Tax Exemption for Homestead Property," Florida Department of Revenue.

This means you potentially get to knock $50,000 off the assessed value of your home for tax assessment purposes as soon as you're homesteaded.

Of the two benefits, the "Save Our Homes" assessment cap will have the biggest impact over the long term, but it takes a few years to really appreciate the effects. We've seen people move to Florida and initially buy a smaller home. That way, they can keep their property taxes low until they've divested themselves from their former state. Then, once they've established residency in Florida completely, they trade the smaller home for something a bit bigger.

The element of creditor protection is huge as well, and it's written into the Florida state constitution. That makes it a benefit that is almost certainly going to stick around. There are additional provisions for disabled veterans and first responders as well, who get an even larger property tax exemption beyond the standard homestead exemption.

In order to enjoy this benefit during the current year, you have to *file for the homestead exemption by March 1 and also have become a Florida resident by December 31st of the prior year.* If you file after this date, you can't apply it until the following tax year. Filing is done through your local county government office.

However, you will have to terminate your northern homestead property tax exemption, and any associated exemptions, if you have them. Here, we recommend contacting your local county's tax office up north. Florida's feathers could get ruffled if you're benefiting from a homestead exemption up north and then also claiming one down here. That's double-dipping, and it's a big no-no. States communicate with one another nowadays, and you have to pick one or the other.

Of course, in some states, this is a non-issue, because they don't offer a homestead exemption, or one that is all that noteworthy. However, there are a few notable examples. For example, your property taxes in Michigan and Indiana can potentially increase substantially if you forfeit your current homestead exemption, so if you're maintaining a home in your northern state, you need to be aware of how it might impact you. This is where it becomes a good idea to meet with someone who can conduct a quantitative analysis, using data from a local property appraiser in your former state and data from a local property appraiser here in Florida to determine what your actual property tax benefit will be.

Will the benefits of moving to Florida outweigh the loss of benefits from leaving your former state? You may discover that you will lose some of the property tax benefits in the short term but that eventually, over a number of years, the cumulative effect of Florida's assessment cap will eventually make it worthwhile. Considering homestead alone, how long will you have to wait to tip the scales in your favor? Five years? Ten years? Twenty-five? These are the kinds of questions that a quantitative analysis and a set of underlying assumptions can answer for you. Our team regularly works with teams of professionals like yours to provide these to individuals as part of their considerations in a move to Florida.

At the same time, as we've said before, you need to consider the qualitative value of the move, beyond merely getting a bigger property tax break. This is the personal, emotional side of making the move. A homestead exemption won't do you much good if you or your family doesn't *want* to make the move, has a much stronger attachment to your northern home, or has personal and business ties that you're not willing to break.

PORTABILITY

So what happens when you have a property established as your homestead but you want to move to a new property? What if you decide to relocate to a nicer house on the other side of town or wish to downsize? Can you homestead the new property? The answer is yes, and the process is called "portability."

Portability allows most Florida residents to transfer their "Save Our Homes" benefit from their previous homestead to a new homestead, which may lower the tax assessment for the new homestead. To transfer the benefit, you first have to establish a homestead exemption for your new home within three years of January 1 in the year you left your previous homestead. Then you must file a Transfer of Homestead Assessment Difference by March 1.[20]

OTHER HOMESTEAD CONSIDERATIONS

The creditor protection aspect of the homestead exemption in Florida typically applies to an individual or couples holding a home in joint tenancy. However, if the home is held in the title of a revocable trust, then the issue is a little cloudy, and the Florida Supreme Court has not yet made a clear ruling on this. We've found that the advice of northern attorneys and Florida attorneys is often very different.

In our experience of working closely with estate planning attorneys in Florida, we've seen it's more common to have "tenants by entirety," which is a way for married couples to

---

20 "Save Our Homes Assessment Limitation and Portability Transfer," Florida Department of Revenue.

hold equal interest in a property as well as survivorship rights, because it keeps the property out of probate and provides more creditor protection. Then, upon the first death, they can update the property to the survivor's revocable trust. Again, it's always wise and encouraged to consult with a Florida-based estate planning attorney who knows your planning so you can figure out the best way to title your home.

CHAPTER FOUR

A SHIELD FOR YOUR HARD-EARNED ASSETS

IF YOU'RE LOOKING for tax savings in Florida, then chances are, you probably have a healthy income, or you've built up a nice estate. In fact, wealthy Americans are flocking to Florida and Texas, with both states gaining over 400,000 new residents in 2022.[21]

---

21 Ty Roush, "Florida and Texas Led the Nation in Population Growth This Year—While New York Had Largest Decline," *Forbes*, December 22, 2022, https://www.forbes.com/sites/tylerroush/2022/12/22/florida-and-texas-led-the-nation-in-population-growth-this-year---while-new-york-had-largest-decline/?sh=7d91e6876cd9/.

CHAPTER FOUR

THE TOP TEN MOVING DESTINATIONS

1. Texas
2. Florida
3. North Carolina
4. Georgia
5. Arizona
6. South Carolina
7. Tennessee
8. Washington
9. Utah
10. Idaho[22]

It makes sense that so many people are coming to Florida. No one wants to lose an unfair amount of what they've worked so hard to build. Now, if you're in that boat, then you're also probably rather savvy when it comes to your money, as demonstrated by the fact that you've been able to build up such a generous asset base. So, you're probably not the type to just leave all of your money for state governments to pick apart, not without first making some wise decisions to minimize the impact of what you keep at the end of the day. And, based on our experience with hundreds of clients,

---

22 "Growth in U.S. Population Shows Early Indication of Recovery amid COVID-19 Pandemic," press release no. CB22-214, December 22, 2022, United States Census Bureau, https://www.census.gov/newsroom/press-releases/2022/2022-population-estimates.html.

there's a good chance that this is a large part of what's driving your thought process as you consider a move to Florida.

However, the government isn't the only entity you have to worry about. A single creditor event could take your assets away from you without warning. Think about it: you could get in a car accident tomorrow and find yourself party to a lawsuit. Or the trouble might not even begin during your lifetime. After you're gone, your primary heir could go through a tough divorce, and suddenly a lot of the assets you left for your children and generations to come will be in danger of going to the divorcing spouse.

Obviously, you can't control every circumstance, and there's no failsafe way to protect every dollar you've acquired. However, as a smart and savvy person with a healthy net worth, it is important to do all you can to protect your assets from creditors in our highly litigious culture. Can Florida help you do this? As it turns out, yes, it can. Florida provides some very strong creditor protections—we believe among the strongest in the nation—which create what we call "Sunshine State Shield" to help protect your assets from creditors.

ALL KINDS OF PROTECTION FROM CREDITORS

We've already talked about one important aspect of this creditor shield: Florida's homestead exemption. For many affluent people, their primary residence makes up a large portion of their overall assets, so being able to protect the value of their home is a huge part of protecting their overall net worth. However, Florida provides some other forms of creditor protection as well.

First, the cash value of any life insurance policy you have is also excluded from attachment, garnishment, or any legal process of any creditor. Let's suppose your business has a really bad year, and some creditors come after you. You have a life insurance policy worth $100,000. Well, in Florida, the creditors most likely can't touch that policy. You could even take out a loan against the cash value of your life insurance policy, and that loan would also be protected from creditors.[23]

Second, most (but not all) annuities are protected from creditors in Florida as well, and the cash value of annuities is generally exempt from creditor claims.

Third, retirement accounts are also generally protected from creditors. This includes, for example, Traditional and Roth IRAs, as well as 401(k) and 403(b) plans. Pensions are also usually protected.[24] Bear in mind, distributions or withdrawals from a retirement account are *not* protected.

Other types of accounts that are protected from creditors include Health Savings Accounts (HSAs), qualified tuition programs for your children's future college tuition, and even some inherited retirement accounts. That's a pretty good deal. So, if you find yourself in trouble with creditors, there's a good chance that your primary residence, your retirement accounts, your life insurance, HSAs, and your child's tuition program are all going to be protected in the state of Florida.

Now, other assets could indeed be exposed to creditors, so you will want to look at additional protection. For example, there's a titling designation known as "tenancy by entirety," which is a way for married couples to hold equal interest in an asset and potentially add an element of creditor protection.

---

23   Bishop L. Toups, "Protecting Your Assets in Florida: Which Assets Are Protected by Florida Law?" Daily, Montfort & Toups, June 20, 2021, https://taxattorneydaily.com/estate-planning/florida-law-for-protecting-assets/.

24   Section 222.21 of Florida Statutes.

There are other ways to fortify your creditor protection. Strong homeowner's insurance, auto insurance, and umbrella coverage can fill in the gaps. Again, it's a good idea to meet with a financial expert to see what your creditor exposures are, but Florida really does give you a great advantage compared to many other states. You'll have more defense for your assets, which can make a big difference if something tragic happens or things go awry.

ARE YOU REALLY AT RISK?

If you're headed into retirement, you might not really feel like you're at risk from creditors. Do you really need extra protection? All of the risk happens earlier in life, doesn't it, when you're chasing a career? We had a client tell us, "Hey, I had plenty of creditor risk when I was an entrepreneur and a restaurant owner, but I'm past all of that now. I'm comfortable and retired. The risk is behind me."

As a gentle reminder, we live in a litigious, "sue happy" society, and the affluent often become bigger targets because of their wealth. You could be driving down the street tomorrow and cause a severe accident. You could hire someone to work on your house, and suddenly they fall off the roof and injure themselves. In either case, there's a good chance that the first thing they're going to do is meet with an attorney and look at the possibility of compensation. And that attorney is going to look at all of your assets to see what they can claim and attach. They're not just going to sue you for the medical costs. In many cases, they're going to attempt to sue you for every penny they can get their hands on, and you just never know what the courts will decide.

Even if you're retired or live a "low risk" lifestyle, if you have substantial assets, a good income, or a high net worth, then the risk is *never* really behind you. You always need protection, and in Florida, you at least have some decent protections provided by law for many of your assets. There are also some specific asset protection maneuvers you can make, such as setting up an irrevocable trust, which enables you to gift money through a structure that provides a massive shield against creditors.

Consider the following common "black swan" events. How many of them could happen to you?

- Divorce
- Automobile or boat accident
- Accident at the home
- Accident on the job
- Illness
- Economic downturn
- Business failure / Bankruptcy
- Unexpected death

Whether you're aware of your risk or not, don't you want the peace of mind that your hard-earned assets will be passed down to your children and not taken away by a litigious individual, entity, or a divorcing spouse? And if your heirs are party to a lawsuit, don't you want to protect your assets for their benefit as well? Accidents happen. Marriages fall apart. Sometimes, the worst comes to pass. Florida, at least, provides some additional protections, which can give you a leg up.

Additionally, we often encourage people to make sure they have adequate *umbrella coverage*. If you're not familiar with it, umbrella insurance provides protection beyond the existing limits and coverages of your other insurance policies. Let's suppose you have a $300,000 liability to your automobile policy. You get in a wreck, and the person you hit successfully sues you for $500,000. That's more than your auto policy will cover, so who is going to make up the difference?

Normally, the plaintiff is going to go after your assets to make up the difference, but umbrella coverage fills in that gap. Additionally, the insurance company will also fight the case for you because they don't want to pay out more than they have to. Umbrella coverage is generally pretty affordable, possibly little more than a few hundred dollars a year per $1 million of coverage, but this depends on your unique situation. It's a relatively inexpensive solution when looking to protect assets that exceed the coverage of your existing policies.

If you want to be conservative, you could get just enough umbrella coverage to cover the value of all of your assets minus those components that are protected from creditors, and in Florida, quite a few of your assets will be protected from creditors. Let's suppose you have a net worth of $10 million, but $5 million of that is in your primary residence. In that case, you would want to consider at least $5 million of umbrella coverage. Again, you can talk to a financial planner and insurance advisor about this as part of your overall changing financial health and well-being.

Another way to protect yourself in Florida is through something called a "dynasty trust," which ensures you can transfer wealth through multiple generations while minimizing your exposure to transfer taxes.[25] At one time, a dynasty trust in Florida could last as long as 360 years, but recently, the state extended it to a breathtaking 1,000 years! Yes, your

---

25 Will Kenton, "Dynasty Trust: Definition, Purposes, How It Works, and Tax Rules," Investopedia, last updated October 21, 2022, https://www.investopedia.com/terms/d/dynasty-trust.asp.

assets can potentially be protected in a trust for up to 1,000 years in the state of Florida.

Florida Governor Ron DeSantis signed a bill in May of 2022 that increased Florida's statutory rule against perpetuities period to 1,000 years. The new rule applies to trusts created on or after July 1, 2022.[26]

Honestly, that's hard to imagine. Can you imagine your assets moving from generation to generation for a thousand years? That's some incredibly strong asset protection, and the Sunshine State respects that.

Ultimately, however you and your financial planner decide to do it, Florida provides you with many options for shielding your assets from creditors. If you have a lot of assets, and you hope to pass them on to your heirs, Florida may be the place for you.

---

26 "Current Developments in Estate Planning and Business Law: June 2022," WealthCounsel, June 17, 2022, https://info.wealthcounsel.com/blog/current-developments-in-estate-planning-and-business-law-june-2022.

CHAPTER FIVE

SETTLING DOWN IN THE SUNSHINE STATE

AT SOME POINT, after you've done your homework, carefully weighed the pros and cons, and reviewed the quantitative and qualitative aspects, you are ready to commit to the decision of becoming a resident. Getting to this point might actually feel pretty anticlimactic because you can get a lot of the actual paperwork and items done fairly quickly at your local government office to secure your residency. You're probably not going to suffer the same kind of experience that you might get from visiting the Department of Motor Vehicles up north and spending weeks in their office.

In fact, it's usually a very straightforward process of going from desk to desk at your local Florida county government office, and we've seen some people do it in record time. As it turns out, there are namely five things you need to do to become a Florida resident. We call them "The Fundamental Five."

CHAPTER FIVE

THE FUNDAMENTAL FIVE

First, you need to spend a reasonable amount of time in Florida. You have to make sure you enjoy being here before you commit to living here. There is no technical "days test" for how many days you must spend in Florida, but you should be spending a good amount of the year here—and if you're higher risk, the more days the better. Make sure you love this state, and be sure you want to build a new life for yourself in Florida before you do anything else.

Second, register your vehicles here. Why wouldn't you want a Florida license plate on a vehicle you're driving in Florida? The official requirement is that you have a minimum of one car registered in Florida. If you have multiple, it isn't necessarily a requirement to register them all with Florida. However, if you are at a higher risk of an audit (more about that later), we recommend that you register more (or all) of your vehicles in Florida. Remember, when you register your vehicles, that includes both cars *and* boats.

Third, get a Florida driver's license like any normal resident would. Again, if you're going to live here, why wouldn't you want to have a local driver's license? More than that, by registering your license and vehicles in Florida, you provide proof of intent to your northern state that you are a Floridian.

If you're a couple and you're both becoming Floridians, both of you will need to get Florida licenses. Don't worry—there is no driver's test, only a quick sight test. The government office typically takes your northern license and clips the top corner and gives it back to you. Then you get a newly minted Florida license at the office right then and there!

Fourth, while you're at it, you should register to vote in Florida, again right there at your county government office.

Finally, and perhaps most importantly, consider filing a document called a Declaration of Domicile. Each county in Florida has its own version of this document, but its purpose is to make your intention clear. You are officially declaring yourself (and your spouse, if applicable) to be a Floridian, signing off on it with the document that is then notarized and recorded at your local county government center.

If your former state ever questions whether or not you really intend to become a Florida resident, the Declaration of Domicile will make it as clear as Florida's blue waters what your intentions are—as formal Florida residents.

Here's a sample of a Declaration of Domicile, in this case from Collier County, which is publicly available on their website:[27]

DECLARATION OF DOMICILE

To the Clerk of the Circuit Court (County Comptroller) of Collier County, Florida.

This is my declaration of domicile in the State of Florida that I am filing this day in accordance and in conformity with Section 222.17, Florida Statutes.

FOR DOMICILIARIES OF THE STATE OF FLORIDA:

I hereby declare that I reside in and maintain a place of abode at:

_____
(street and number)

_____, Florida
(city and county)

which place of abode I recognize and intend to maintain as my permanent home and, if I maintain another place or places of abode in some other state or states, I hereby declare that my above-described residence and abode in the State of Florida constitutes my predominant and principal home, and I intend to continue it permanently as such. I am, at the time of making this declaration, a bona fide resident of the State of Florida residing at:

_____
(street and number)

_____, Florida
(city and county)

I formerly resided at:

_____
(street and number)

_____
(city, county and state)

and the place or places where I maintain another or other place or places of abode are as follows: (Here list street address, city, county, and state of any other place or places of abode.)

_____
(Signature)

_____
(Print Name)

Sworn to and subscribed before me this _____ of _____, _____.

Crystal K. Kinzel
Clerk of the Circuit Court & Comptroller

_____
(Signature of Deputy Clerk)

_____
(Signature of Notary Public, State of Florida)

_____
(Printed Name of Deputy Clerk)

_____
(Print, type or stamp commissioned name of Notary Public)

Personally known _____ or Produced Identification _____
(Check One)
Type of Identification produced _____

(See reverse side for Domiciliaries of States Other than the State of Florida)

---

[27] https://collierclerk.com/wp-content/uploads/Declaration-of-Domicile.pdf.

CHAPTER FIVE

THE FUNDAMENTAL FIVE

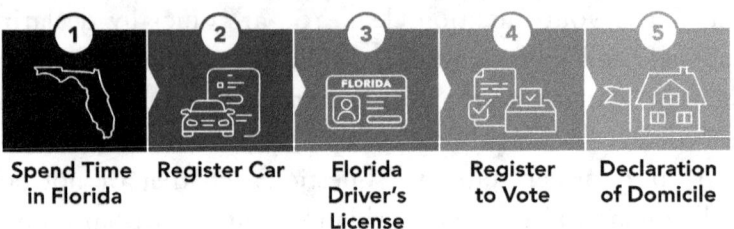

SO MANY THINGS TO DO

While these are the "Fundamental Five," there's actually a whole list of other things that can help your case. Remember, if you pay a lot of taxes in your former state, then odds are you're going to be a greater target when you leave—and the bigger a target you are, the more likely you are to be looked into or audited. The more you can do to prove your intent, the stronger your case will be. This is all the more true if you own a business.

So what are some additional things you can do to establish your residency in Florida?

One simple thing you can do is to *update your estate planning documents* so they reflect your Florida residency. You can also update your bank account statements, investment account statements, and other financial documents. Some states will ask about these things, but even if they don't, why would you want financial documents of any kind to go to your former state anyway? These are important documents, and you'd typically want them to be sent to your primary home.

If you dust off your foundational estate planning documents—revocable trust, will, power of attorney—the first paragraph will usually mention the county and state you are a resident of in your former state. You're now a Floridian, but it is important to eliminate any confusion or gray areas among the states over your estate when that day arrives. And if your northern state has a state estate tax, this is all the more important.

Some northern states, in the event of an audit, will check to see if you have a *safe deposit box* in a northern state. We certainly understand the rationale. Why would you keep sentimental items, valuables, or important documents in a state where you no longer live? Wouldn't you want them near your home or main residence?

It's also a good idea to begin working with professionals such as an estate planning attorney, financial advisor, and accountant who are located in Florida. Remember, optics are important. You've made the move to Florida and established a team of local professionals to guide you. Is this a requirement? No. However, if all of your professionals are located in your northern state, some will wonder if you're truly a Floridian.

Here are some other ideas and methods that are highly encouraged to help you weigh Florida residency in your favor:

- Use your Florida address on your tax return and file your federal tax return properly through the nearest IRS Regional Centers for Florida: Atlanta, Georgia, or Austin, Texas. Please engage your CPA here and ensure that your return is no longer routed through your northern IRS Regional Center.
- File a final tax return in your former state (engage your CPA), unless you continue to receive taxable income in that state (largely from tangible sources such as a farm, rental home, or commercial building).
- Celebrate some important family occasions in Florida (and get pictures/video). Maybe post some of them on

social media, so the date and time of these events can be verified.
- Change registrations and update mailing addresses for the following:
  - Bank accounts
  - Investment accounts
  - Social Security (www.ssa.gov)
  - Important documents
  - Boat registration
  - Professional licenses
  - Utility statements
- Transfer your family possessions, artwork, and heirlooms to Florida.
- Transact business from Florida, or work from home in Florida.
- Notify your Property and Casualty Insurance carriers of your changing residency.
- Notify your health insurance carrier.
- Join local clubs, religious institutions, and volunteer.
- Ensure non-residency on northern organizations and licensures.
- Volunteer for charities in Florida and in your community.
- Establish relationships with local and regional Florida professionals.
  - Estate planning attorney
  - Financial advisor
  - Accountant
  - Physician and Veterinarian
- If you happen to have a northern safe deposit box, close it and put the contents in a safe. Or, transfer the contents to a new safe deposit box in Florida.
- If applicable, enroll your children in a Florida school.

Look, you're not doing all of these things in order to convince Florida to let you become a resident. Florida is going to welcome you with open arms. Rather, you're doing all of this in order to prove to your northern state that you are indeed moving your residence to Florida. Moreover, these are "normal" things that any resident of a state would do.

By taking *objective* steps, like getting a Florida driver's license, as well as the above *subjective* steps, such as getting involved in a local organization, you create a strong case that you really are a resident of Florida. The Fundamental Five are the most important steps, but anything else you can do to bolster your case will help.

IT ONLY TAKES AN AFTERNOON

Fortunately, Florida wants to make the process of becoming a resident as easy and efficient as possible for you. Just contact your local government center, and they will guide you through the process. In fact, you can probably get most of this done in an afternoon, especially The Fundamental Five. We've heard of people knocking out everything they need to do there in forty-five minutes!

First, visit the nearest government center. Then, log into your various financial accounts online and update your address. Set a meeting with your estate planning attorney (we heavily advise engaging a *Florida-based* professional in this capacity) to amend your documents, so they reflect your Florida residency.

If your former state ever questions you, you'll be able to say, "Hey, my team of financial professionals are all in Florida. All of my documents say I'm in Florida. I've moved my safe deposit boxes to Florida. My financial advisors, attorneys, and primary care physician are all in Florida. How much more do I have to do to prove I really do live here?"

CHAPTER FIVE

Think about it from the perspective of a northern state government. If a taxpayer claims they're moving to Florida, but all of their professional relationships and financial accounts remain up north, it's going to look fishy. Of course, they may be more likely to look into that person's situation because it seems like they're just trying to game the system. Your job is to do everything you can to protect yourself from these kinds of questions and concerns. Make it crystal clear that you're actually establishing your residence in Florida, and don't leave any uncertainty for your former state to use as leverage against you.

While the whole process of moving is usually a fairly straightforward process, you may have some complications. For example, if you own rental property or a producing farm in your northern state, then you might still be subject to state income tax on those assets. Every case is unique, so coordinate with your Florida-based estate planning attorney and your CPA to make sure you know what you're dealing with.

HOW MANY DAYS PER YEAR?

Now, here's an important question. How much time do you actually have to spend in Florida in order to count as a resident? You may have homes in multiple states that you like to spend time in, so how many days per year will you have to live in your Florida home to make a legitimate claim to being a Floridian?

The answer we typically say in most instances is, conservatively, 185 days (technically, in some states it is 181, 182, or 183, but we like to be extra safe and round up). No matter how many homes you own in various states, plan to be outside of the borders of your former state for at least 185 days per year. Now, bear in mind, this isn't a Florida requirement. Florida has no minimum number of days that you have to live in-state to prove you're a resident. Again, this is about proving to your northern state that you really have moved away.

Quite frankly, you don't have to be in Florida during those 185 days. You just have to prove that you're not living in your northern state during that time. So you can visit your kids in Colorado, take three weeks of vacation in the Carolinas, or whatever else you want to do. You just have to be provably *outside* of your northern state at least 185 days per year (in some northern states, it's 181 days). Technically, you don't have to be in Florida during that time, and Florida itself has no "days test."

TaxBird

There are apps that can actually help you stay on top of this. One example is called TaxBird, and it's a residency tracker that tracks your geolocation every hour and every day using your cell phone location and credit card purchases.[28] While it may seem a bit Big Brother, it can provide further proof that you really do live in Florida. Just remember, every hour you spend in your former northern state will count against you. Even if you're flying back to Minneapolis and land at 11 o'clock at night, the state will consider you as being in that state a full day or "contact point."

If you are to be audited, the northern state government can ask for cell phone records proving where you've been, as each text, email, or call you make from that phone pings off the closest cell phone tower (generally located about a

---

28   https://www.taxbird.com/.

mile away). TaxBird provides this information for you so you can adjust your schedule accordingly to bolster your claim of Florida residency. More than that, if you're ever audited by your former state, the app data can provide concrete proof of where you spent most of your time.

Some people prefer to keep track of their location using a simple Excel spreadsheet or even just a pad of paper, but anything can be written down on paper. The app provides actual geolocation data, which is, in our opinion, far more defensible than just some notes you've written yourself, and again, anything you can do to bolster your claim of being a Florida resident will help you when your northern state starts asking questions.

But you need more than just an app. When it's time to make the actual move, you need a team of talented professionals. Let's look at the key players that contribute to creating a winning team.

CHAPTER SIX

MAKING YOUR MOVE

COORDINATING YOUR TEAM OF PROFESSIONALS

Making the decision to move to Florida is half the battle. We've seen people struggle with the decision for a long time, but when they finally decide to make the move, the actual process goes pretty smoothly. It's a big decision and getting to that point isn't always easy.

WHO ARE YOUR TEAM MEMBERS?

Sometimes the *qualitative* side outweighs the *quantitative* side of the equation. It might make perfect sense financially, but not personally. And sometimes, a person who is on the fence qualitatively might be tipped in one direction or the other when the financial reality becomes clear. For someone with a high net worth, this isn't a decision that can be made lightly, so it needs to be made carefully.

To do that, we recommend bringing together a team of professionals who will "run the numbers" and provide you with all of the hard data you need to make the clearest possible decision. Your financial advisor, estate planner, and CPA should be able to give you an estimated dollar amount of savings given the applicability of three taxes (state income tax, state estate tax, homestead tax benefits) and how much money could be saved by becoming a Floridian.

Is there a point for you at which the financial benefit would outweigh the costs? Possibly. For most people, we find this to be the case.

At the very least, you can make an educated decision based on hard numbers rather than crossing your fingers and hoping for the best. By working with a team of professionals who can conduct the analyses, you will get all of the information you need and come to the conclusion that makes the most sense for you.

Once your decision is made, that team can then help you plan the move and execute it by providing you with all of the tools and resources you need to get all of your finances, estate planning, and tax planning in order.

This smart investment on the front end is the best way to ensure that you have all the documents you need right at your fingertips, and you have the right people to guide you through the process quickly and easily.

WHO'S THE QUARTERBACK?

Now, once you have a team of professionals to guide you through the decision and process, it's important to get buy-in from all of them. You want a team that is united and working toward the same goals. If your accountant's viewpoints are conflicting with your financial advisor or estate planner, then it's going to be a lot harder to work together. To prevent that, we recommend appointing one individual as a quarterback to keep all of the other team members on the same page.

The quarterback for your team needs to be someone who understands your context so they can help you put together a comprehensive plan and an outline of what's important to you both quantitatively and qualitatively. Let's suppose you set a financial goal to make a certain amount of money per year during retirement for thirty years. To do that, you need to outline your assets and determine how they're titled, what their value is, and how this all works in the context of your liabilities, insurance, tax, and estate needs. In most cases where you have an ongoing advisory relationship, a trusted financial advisor should be employing this review as part of your ongoing client services.

Additionally, once you've outlined all of this, you need to figure out how your plan is going to be affected by moving to Florida. That will require working with an investment advisor representative, accountant, estate planner, and possibly a property casualty insurance advisor. We recommend selecting someone to quarterback all of these people so they work together well.

Getting your financial picture in a clear and understandable order can seem overwhelming, especially if you have a complex financial situation, and working with multiple people can only add to the complexity. By appointing someone to quarterback the process, you can keep all of these people and all of these pieces moving together toward the finish line.

Before you can appoint a quarterback for your team, however, you need to identify all of the players you need on your team. Let's look a little closer at the players on a winning team.

CHAPTER SIX

YOUR WINNING PLAYERS

So, what kinds of experts should you bring together to guide you through the process of establishing your residency in Florida? Above all, we recommend working with a *financial advisor*, a *Florida estate planning attorney*, a *CPA*, and an *insurance advisor*. One of these individuals should also be the "quarterback," and in most cases, in our opinion, the person best suited to do this will be your financial advisor as they typically have a broad perspective of your overall financial scenario.

If you're planning to formally become a Florida resident, we believe it's a good practice to find a good primary care physician wherever you're moving, and you might even find a local veterinarian if you have pets. This makes it easier to transfer your medical records to your new home, and ensures that any treatment continues without interruption. And if you have beloved pets, it ensures the same thing for them. Now, your medical records and veterinary records, in our experience, aren't usually things that your former state will look at when they're considering an audit, but the more you can do to reinforce the idea that you are indeed a Florida resident, the better it will be—and the stronger your case will be, if it comes to that.

Often, when we first start working with a client, we discover that they haven't even looked at their estate documents in ten to fifteen years, so this is the perfect time to revisit them. Work with an estate planning attorney and use the opportunity to ensure that everything is the way you want it to be. Otherwise, the government will make a plan for you through the probate process.

This is also as good a time as ever to revisit your investment portfolio with your financial advisor and make sure you're set up to meet your future goals. If you have a concentration of municipal bonds in your portfolio issued by municipalities from your previous state of residence, it might be a good idea to revisit your portfolio to see if there are opportunities to smartly diversify it. Maybe you want to put your money into different bonds across the country rather than just concentrating them within the boundaries of a single state. In Florida, most municipal bond interest income is double tax-exempt when it comes to both federal and state income tax, regardless of the state of issue; however, it may be subject to alternative minimum tax (AMT) depending on your unique situation. As always, it's important to understand your different risks and how they are being managed.

We prefer to collaborate closely with our client's team of professionals to ensure that they're taking advantage of long-term planning opportunities. For example, a market downturn might present an opportunity to work closely with your financial advisor and estate attorney as you consider gifting appreciated stock to your kids outright or to an irrevocable trust. You may want to coordinate a discussion with your financial advisor and accountant to discuss a Roth IRA conversion during a stock market drawdown. Open lines of communication amongst your team of professionals will help you capitalize on opportunities to strengthen your scenario in the long term.

You can also look for new ways to protect your accounts in Florida. In other words, use this move as motivation to evaluate *everything* in your finances. Work with a financial advisor in Florida because they're going to be the most familiar with local opportunities. Let them open up the proverbial hood and take a look inside your investment portfolio. Besides helping you make the move and changing your documents accordingly, they may also have some fresh ideas for improving your planning and portfolio to more effectively achieve your long-term financial goals.

A QUESTION OF TIMING

Once you have a team of experts, get each of them involved in the decision-making process because they're each going to bring an important perspective, and together, they will help to cover all of your financial bases. One important question is timing. When should you make the move? Likely, the best person to answer this question will be a tax advisor or CPA. They will tell you when to file your taxes and when you need to complete and file other paperwork.

For example, we met with an individual not long ago who wanted to move to Florida late in the year. He was ready, mentally and emotionally, to pull the trigger, but when we met with his team, it became clear that it would make more sense for him to wait until early the following year. He didn't have the financial structure in place to "get away clean" from his northern state, and his team was able to point this out to him.

Of course, if you really want to move to Florida late in the year, consider checking with your tax advisor about possibly prorating the year from a tax perspective. A CPA can help you with all of these timing-related questions so you at least know what you're dealing with, but if putting off the move just a little longer will make your life a lot easier, then we can't see any reason not to wait.

You don't know what you don't know. That's why it's so important to have a team of professionals working together and vested in understanding what you're looking to undertake in becoming long-term Florida residents. Each team member can focus on specific areas of your strategy, while the quarterback calls the plays and keeps the whole team moving forward. And you get to stand on the sidelines and enjoy watching them reach your goals quickly and efficiently.

CHAPTER SEVEN

ESTATE PLANNING ESSENTIALS

ESTATE PLANNING IS essential for every individual and every family, *especially* for those who have a high net worth. The more you've built and acquired over the years, the more important it becomes to ensure that you have a solid plan in place to deal with the eventual disposition of your assets, liabilities, insurance, and even the guardianship of children and pets. Without a plan, the transfer of your assets will be handled by the government, and they're liable to make some decisions that you (or your heirs) wouldn't like.

Maybe you already have an estate planner in your northern state, someone you've worked with for years who really knows your business, but it's worthwhile to speak to a Florida-based estate planning attorney if you intend to move here. Your existing planner is probably more familiar with the state you're leaving. There are some nuances of Florida law that they may not understand, and it's worthwhile to partner with a trusted estate planner in Florida that deals primarily with law in the Sunshine State.

We recommend making sure that the person you speak to in Florida is a full-time estate planning attorney, not someone who does estate planning as a part of their practice. Your assets, your heirs, and your future are too important to entrust them to someone who might not specialize in this field. Of course, this is just common sense. If you needed knee surgery, you wouldn't go to a general practitioner to perform the surgery! You'd go to a specialist, an orthopedic surgeon who does knee surgeries all day long and knows the ins and outs of the procedure.

In the same way, you want to work with someone who specializes full-time in estate planning in Florida, because they're less likely to miss something important. And if they're based in Florida, then they're going to be well-acquainted with Florida state laws and regulations. This is the perfect time to do a full refresh of everything in your estate plan, taking all local opportunities into consideration.

Make sure you work with your Florida-based estate planning attorney to update *every document* to reflect your Florida residency while you're at it. You don't want some important estate document to still list your former state as your residence just because you or your estate planner forgot to go through everything. And when you pass, you don't want some northern state to show up and try to claim part of your assets, using your own documents against your heirs simply because you failed to revisit everything:

"Hey, this document right here says their home state was New York, so let's lay claim to a piece of the estate for taxes!"

Fortunately, with a bit of proactive planning and regular upkeep, you can rest easy that your hard-earned money will be passed along as you see fit based on your intentions. And your move to Florida is the perfect opportunity to go through everything and make sure it's all in order. A good Florida estate planner will customize your plan within the scope of the law to best achieve your goals long after you're gone.

This is important for a few reasons.

AVOIDING PROBATE

If you don't explicitly state who your beneficiaries are, then the government is going to step in and do it for you. That means your estate will go through probate court, and this can become doubly complicated if your northern state tries to claim you as a resident.

Bear in mind, probate is public, so everyone is going to know about your personal business. First of all, a notice of your death will be filed publicly and possibly published in the newspaper. This is intended to give creditors notice so they can try to collect on any outstanding debts at the time of your passing, but it could also bring long-lost relatives and former friends out of the woodwork to try to make a claim.

While your beneficiaries and heirs can assert their rights at the beginning of the probate process, the distribution of your assets can be contested. Do you really want your children, heirs, creditors, and others squabbling over your money after you're gone?

Now, you may say, "I already have an estate plan. I've had one for years. Nobody's going to contest anything." However, unless you take the time to go through all of your estate documents when you move to Florida, you might overlook something, fail to update some paperwork, or fail to take advantage of some opportunity. As a result, you could introduce problems for your heirs that weren't there previously.

Probate isn't cheap. Typically, it will cost anywhere between

2 and 7 percent of the value of the estate. Think about that. A million-dollar estate might wind up costing $50,000 in probate fees, with the money going to the court, to attorneys, to researchers. Even then, your assets can be held up in court for months, a year, or even longer, before they are ultimately passed along to your heirs. And ultimately, who knows what the court will decide on the direction with respect to your assets?

This is not a game you want to play, so use this opportunity to get it right. The types of assets that are subject to probate are generally individually named or solely owned assets in your name. This includes things like an investment account or a home titled in your sole name. Generally, this is an asset that doesn't have a listed beneficiary or direction on it after the death of the owner. Keep in mind that with only a will, said assets will likely be subject to probate.

There are also some assets that are not subject to probate, but it's best to clarify this with your Florida estate planning attorney. Assets that aren't subject to probate generally have the following titling:

- Joint tenants with rights of survivorship*
- Tenants by entirety* (Tenants by entirety is used more frequently in some states than others. In Florida, it is the default form of co-ownership in real estate for married couples.)
- Community property (applicable only in certain states)
- Revocable (living) trust
- Individual account with a "Transfer on Death" or "Payable on Death" designation
- Traditional or Roth IRA (or other retirement plan, e.g., 401(k)) with a beneficiary designation
- Annuity and life insurance with a beneficiary designation
- Household goods to immediate family members

Joint accounts can be subject to probate on the death of the second account holder.

The full review of your estate plan provides the perfect time to make sure that you know how your assets are going to be distributed after your passing. Your family situation might have changed over the years since you first put your plan together, so here's your chance to make sure that the plan fulfills your current expectations and wishes.

Look at the distributions to your spouse, children, extended family, charities, friends, and acquaintances. Are they up to date, reflecting your current life, relationships, and desires? Use this opportunity to tweak, adjust, and update your financial legacy, so you know how your assets are going to be invested, used, or enjoyed once you're gone.

To do that, your financial advisor should have an outline of all of your current assets, ensuring that your assets are properly titled to keep them out of probate so they pass to your heirs or beneficiaries efficiently and quickly. Update all of the information on your documents and make any necessary changes to your listed beneficiaries or owners. It's possible that some people have passed away, or they're no longer a part of your life, since you last visited your estate planning documents. A good estate planning attorney will understand the implications of your assets, financial well-being, family dynamics, and desires in regard to the passing of your estate.

Here are the primary documents that should be considered as part of your estate plan. Please note that *all* of your estate planning documents should reflect you (and your spouse or partner) as Florida residents.

CHAPTER SEVEN

Last Will and Testament

A last will and testament is a document that expresses your final wishes to a court, a judge, and your heirs, but if you want to ensure that those final wishes are carried out, make sure that all of your assets are correctly titled and that the proper documents are readily available. A will doesn't ensure that your assets will avoid going to probate. That's not its purpose. All it is intended to do is provide guidance to the court on the distribution of your assets.

A will is easy to draft, and it's revocable, so you can change it easily at any time. The purpose of your will is to:
- name an executor for your estate,
- provide instruction to the court and others on how your property should be managed after your death,
- name a guardian for your children (of course, this should be known and accepted by the guardian prior to your death),
- provide for any pets you leave behind, and
- give some direction on how taxes and liabilities are to be managed.

Now, bear in mind, your will can't put conditions on the disposition of your assets, so you can't say something like, "My daughter Cindy will get my Lamborghini only when she graduates with a Master's of Fine Arts." Nor can you provide a different direction for the distribution of assets that pass outside of probate and already have a named beneficiary (e.g., assets in a trust, retirement plan distributions to a beneficiary, and jointly held property).

Even so, if you don't have a will yet, this is the perfect opportunity to create one, because it can provide a solid foundation for your estate plan. If you already have one, this is a good time to sit down with an estate planning attorney and revisit it to make sure everything is up to date and fitting to your intentions.

Revocable (or "Living") Trust

A revocable (or "living") trust works similarly to a will, providing instructions on who should get your assets when you die, but unlike a will, it is privately preserved. In other words, while a will is public record, a trust can keep everything in the family.

Additionally, a trust provides instructions for how your assets should be managed both *before* and *after* your death, and it is "revocable" because you can modify it at any time during your life. A trust can help you avoid probate, but unlike a will, it must be "funded," which means any assets that can be updated (e.g., individual or joint accounts) must be updated with a trust title.

A revocable trust helps your heirs in two ways. First, after the grantor's passing the trust then becomes irrevocable and provides *asset protection* from creditors and divorcing spouses. Let's suppose your child is a doctor. She inherits a large piece of your estate, but then she is subject to a malpractice suit because of something that happens in her job. The assets she inherited in your trust typically can't be touched in the judgment against her.

Second, a revocable trust keeps your assets *in the family*. When your time has come, the trust becomes irrevocable, and assets move to your heirs. Your child's ex-spouse can't touch them in a divorce. As with other estate documents, we strongly recommend meeting with an estate planning attorney as part of your move to Florida so they can draft, revise, or update your trust to meet your current needs and expectations. Don't leave it to chance or let your heirs deal with it. Revocable trusts can be a very powerful estate planning tool and can serve your family well for generations to come.

Pour-Over Will

A pour-over will is a legal document that ensures that any of your assets not already included in the trust will be "poured over" to the trust upon your death. The transfer will be automatic, enabling your trustees to administer them as you instruct. If you don't already have a pour-over will, now is as good a time as ever to consider drafting one.

Durable Power of Attorney

A durable power of attorney gives a person you designate the power to handle financial matters on your behalf if you become incapacitated or unable to handle them yourself. This can help keep your estate in good standing no matter what happens to you. Just remember, it is no longer valid once you die. At that point, the executor of your will or your trustee will assume responsibility for your assets.

Healthcare Power of Attorney

A healthcare power of attorney (PoA) document designates someone to act as a surrogate in making healthcare decisions in the event you're unable to make them for yourself. This includes the power to consent to or reject medical treatment, even if the decision results in death. Your estate planning attorney will ensure that your healthcare PoA document complies with HIPAA (Health Insurance Portability and Accountability Act).

Living Will

Similar to your healthcare power of attorney document, a living will provides explicit instructions to your family and physician about what to do when it comes to life-sustaining medical procedures in the event of a terminal illness. Since you may not be able to communicate your intentions at that time, a living will speaks for you. If you don't already have one, it is a good idea to consider it, because it might spare your family from having to make an incredibly difficult decision about "pulling the plug" at the end of your life.

Quitclaim Bill of Sale

A final document that you should consider drafting or revisiting is a *quitclaim bill of sale,* which places your personal property into your trust. This is especially important for items that can't be easily titled, such as jewelry or other prized family heirlooms.

REVISING THE FUTURE

If you've already worked with an estate planning attorney in your northern state, then you probably already have some version of most, if not all, of these documents. However, when you make the move to Florida, you need to revise and update all of your estate plans to reflect your changing life circumstances.

We recommend working with a Florida estate planner, because they can explain the nuances of state law and offer advice for opportunities to update and improve your estate planning documents. You may have some special circumstances that require additional documents, such as a special needs child or other family dynamics. Also, by updating your estate documents, you can further protect yourself and your heirs from a northern state trying to get some of your assets after you're gone. There should be no gray area. Moreover, by hiring a Florida-based estate planner, you further your intentions and gravity about moving your residency to Florida.

Give yourself and your loved ones the peace of mind of knowing that all of your bases have been covered, and your assets will be protected and passed on when you pass. That way, when it's your time to go, you can rest easy knowing that you've provided for your family.

Once your estate plan is updated and revised, it's also a good idea to revisit your investment portfolio to make sure you're taking advantage of every opportunity to build wealth for yourself and future generations.

CHAPTER EIGHT

FINANCIALLY PLANNING AS A FLORIDIAN

WHEN LIFE CHANGES, it's a good idea to revisit your financial plan and update or refine it to better reflect those changes. If you decide to become a Florida resident, that is certainly a big change in your life, and your investments, estate plan, and asset titling should be reviewed. This may be the perfect time to adapt your financial plan to better achieve your goals.

As with your estate plan, take this opportunity to sit down, this time with a Florida financial advisor, and let them raise the hood and look into your investments. They should outline your current and future goals and needs; clarify your assets, liabilities, and insurance; and help you understand and revise your plan. Most importantly, they should have a strong sense of what is important to you and the changes at work in your life. Working with someone in Florida can also help you view your overall financial situation from a Florida perspective, particularly as it pertains to optimizing your investments, asset titling, tax efficiency planning, and creditor protection.

As you revisit your financial plan, your financial advisor can calculate how much you're going to need for monthly spending, annualize it, and extrapolate that number with inflation to figure out what you're going to need in the future. You might find that your monthly income needs are different now that you're in Florida, and the clearer you can get about this number, the easier it will be to work toward reaching it.

For planning purposes, we believe it's a good idea to overestimate your living expenses and assume you're going to live a long life, while also underestimating your investment returns. If your expenses turn out to be lower than planned or investment returns come in higher, you'll be in an even stronger financial position. Err on the side of caution in your expectations so you're positioned to deal with the unpredictable nature of money. Revisit your budget as well because your spending might change with your change of location. The cost of living in Florida might differ from the cost of living in your northern state, and your lifestyle might be different here, as well.

Are your needs and wants different now? First, consider your needs. For example, what are your property taxes and insurance needs in Florida, and how do they compare to your northern state? Then, consider your wants. How will you be splurging on yourself and your family in your new home state? Is it time to buy that nice, new sports car? Will you be joining some local golf club, or buying a bigger home?

After you've identified your needs and wants, clarify your goals, because some of them are likely to have changed as well. With your financial advisor, outline your short-term (under a year), medium-term (one to ten years), or long-term (more than ten years) goals. Are they compatible with one another? Which goals need to take priority? Has the time horizon on some of your goals changed due to your change in residency? How are you tracking?

This refresh of your financial plan also gives you the chance to itemize your resources and see how you're doing at moving toward your goals. Make sure your plan is realistic and try to simplify it, if possible. What is your current level of risk? Does this need to change? Our general thesis in this respect: only take on as much risk with your resources as you need to in order to meet your goals, but no more than that.

You've probably already built up a nice nest egg through years of hard work and discipline, so now is not the time to gamble with it. Are you protected from a catastrophic, or what we call in the financial industry a "black swan," event? Do you and your spouse have different levels of risk appetite? You might have to take on a bit more risk to reach some of your goals. Then, as you get close to those goals, you can dial back the risk. And again, you may need to adjust your level of risk due to circumstances surrounding your move to Florida. It's important to understand expectations.

Now is also a good time to inventory your assets and liabilities, so you know exactly where you stand. If you bring some debt with you to Florida, do you need to adjust your "plan of attack" for paying down those debts? It's also a good opportunity to take a look at all of your insurance policies, including life, long-term care, annuities, personal umbrella insurance, auto, disability, and others. Are there some existing gaps that need to be filled?

Florida is a very tax-friendly state, and, once you officially make the move to the Sunshine State, there are a few ways your investment portfolio can potentially become more tax-efficient. Let's take a look at what they are.

CHAPTER EIGHT

MUNICIPAL BONDS
(STATE, COUNTY, CITY, LOCAL)

When you become a Florida resident, you get easier access to a couple of significant investment benefits. The first are municipal bonds, which are debt securities issued by state, county, city, or local governments to fund various capital projects. When you purchase a municipal bond, you are essentially lending money to the bond issuer with the promise of regular interest payments and an eventual return of the original investment.[29]

Municipal bonds tend to be a highly stable part of an investment portfolio, though they are potentially exposed to fixed-income market conditions, credit risk, interest rate risk, reinvestment risk, inflationary risk, and the forces of supply and demand on price. However, what makes them especially attractive for high-net-worth individuals is that they are usually exempt from federal taxation on interest payments. For complete details on these types of risks, reach out to your financial advisor or visit https://www.raymondjames.com/wealth-management/advice-products-and-services/investment-solutions/fixed-income/pricing-factors/risks-of-bond-investing for more information.

In states with a state income tax, investors are often exempt from paying that tax on interest payments if they hold a municipal bond issued by their state of residence. So, if you lived in New York, you might be exempt from federal and state taxation on interest payments if you hold a municipal

---

29   "Municipal Bonds," Investor.gov, accessed April 6, 2023, https://www.investor.gov/introduction-investing/investing-basics/investment-products/bonds-or-fixed-income-products-0.

bond issued by a New York municipality. There are some exceptions, though in those instances, investors are generally compensated with a higher interest payment. However, this can present an investment risk in this instance as that investor may have all their municipal bonds in this example in New York—akin to "all your eggs in one basket."

Of course, when you invest in a municipal bond as a Florida resident, this is not going to be an issue since there is no state income tax, so you can invest in municipal bonds from theoretically all states in the country, essentially broadening your investment spectrum and adding diversification to your portfolio. The reverse, however, is not true. If a New Yorker invests in a Florida municipal bond, then they are going to be subject to New York state income taxes and potentially local income taxes.

Since you're moving to the state, it might be a good time to consider investing in some municipal bonds issued by other state, county, city, or local governments. Not only do municipal bonds have a historically low default rate compared to other kinds of investments, but they can provide you with a way to create a potentially tax-free monthly income.

Since you're establishing your residence in Florida, you can look for the best opportunities to invest in municipal bonds across the country and typically still enjoy the lack of federal or state taxes on the interest payments. This makes it a whole lot easier to diversify your portfolio, and it puts you at an advantage over people who live in states with income taxes.

The funds that are generated to pay back the principal on a municipal bond generally fall into two categories: general obligation bonds and revenue bonds.

- **General Obligation Bonds**: A general obligation bond's interest payments are generally sourced through the municipality's taxing power and can be generated

by raising taxes. A vote of the citizens is not always required for raising such taxes, which makes it easier for the government to strengthen the credit of these kinds of bonds.
- **Revenue Bonds:** These kinds of bonds are issued for specific projects, such as toll roads, hospitals, and sports stadiums, and the revenue is generated from that project. Since they rely on the success of the underlying project rather than the taxing power of the government, there is generally a higher level of risk. Investors compensate for this risk in the form of higher interest rate payments on the fund they loan to the municipality.

Since Florida has no state income tax and interest income from municipal bonds isn't usually subject to federal taxes, these bonds are a potentially attractive addition to any investment portfolio. Keep in mind, the interest may still be subject to alternative minimum tax (AMT), so be sure to discuss with your tax advisor prior to making any investment decisions.

IRAS AND PENSIONS

There's a second investment advantage that you get from becoming a Florida resident. Any time you take money out of a qualified retirement account (i.e., traditional IRA, 401(k), 403(b), or applicable pensions), it is considered ordinary income, and consequently, it is subject to income taxes. That means federal taxes, of course, but many (*though not all*) northern states also apply state income tax to retirement account distributions. A double hit like that can be painful, but in Florida, you don't have to worry about the second hit.

In fact, we often meet with people looking to move to

Florida before they have to start taking money out of their retirement accounts for this very reason. Generally, you can begin pulling money out at age fifty-nine-and-a-half without incurring a penalty, and then required minimum distributions kick in during your seventies.

Those required distributions are the IRS's way of getting tax dollars out of the pre-tax amount that you put into those accounts, and every year that goes by, those required distributions can potentially become bigger and bigger. All of that money is considered ordinary income, so it's subject to federal and state income taxes.

If you can sidestep paying state income tax on those distributions, then you get to keep more of the money, and if you have a large retirement account, that might be a decent chunk of change over the long run.

Additionally, please keep in mind that qualified retirement accounts are intended to be long-term retirement savings vehicles. As such, early withdrawals, if taken prior to a certain age, may be subject to a 10 percent federal tax penalty on top of the ordinary income taxes you may owe. Matching contributions from your employer may be subject to a vesting schedule. Contributions to a traditional IRA may be tax-deductible depending on the taxpayer's income, tax-filing status, and other factors.

TAXES

Any taxes taken out of your investments are a drag on the portfolio, so anything you can do legally to reduce taxes on your investments is going to be to your advantage. Florida provides you a few more ways to do that. However, it's important to remember that change is inevitable. Elected officials change, governments change, and therefore, policies change.

The world is constantly evolving around us. That means tax situations can change or be amended as well.

Uncle Sam is always going to demand his cut, but because circumstances change, it's important to maintain a relationship with a trusted financial advisor and an accountant who can continually revisit and update your investment portfolio. They have the expertise, and they will stay abreast of ever-changing tax legislation so you don't have to.

Remember, individual retirement accounts (IRAs) and other "qualified" retirement accounts (e.g., 401(k)s and 403(b)s) are typically funded with pre-tax money, so you're likely to pay taxes when they are distributed at ordinary income tax rates. If you've invested in a Roth IRA, then the money was taxed before it was invested, so the IRS has already taken its cut of tax. You get to keep all of the gains for yourself when the money is distributed, provided certain conditions are met.

To help you fully understand the day-to-day tax implications of your investments, here is a brief primer on portfolio taxation.

Capital Gains and Losses

Capital gains and losses represent the positive or negative change in value of an investment since the initial purchase. As long as the investment is held, capital gains or losses should be considered "unrealized" for tax purposes. However, once the investment is sold, they are considered "realized," resulting in potential tax implications if you have a gain.

If you hold an investment for more than a calendar year, you effectively turn a short-term capital gain or loss into a long-term capital gain or loss, which can be taxed at a more advantageous rate.

If your investments do well and produce a lot of unrealized

gains, then you might have to pay capital gains taxes when you realize, sell, or access the funds. That means the better you do, the more tax revenue the government makes!

Then again, the government is also sharing some of the risk, because if you lose money, then they don't get any tax revenue. In fact, if you realize a loss, or end up selling an investment for less than you paid, you can use that loss to offset future gains. Your accountant can help you understand and take advantage of this. You can also talk to a financial advisor, accountant, and estate planning attorney about tax-efficient ways to contribute to charities using funds from your investments to minimize tax obligations.

All of the tax implications of your investment portfolio should be reviewed when you decide to become a Florida resident. We've covered some of the main areas, but there are many other elements of taxation that you can be exposed to, and there are many ways to offset or blunt the impact of taxation on your investments. Now is the perfect time to make sure you're on top of everything, and your financial advisor and accountant can make sure you have a clear understanding of your situation.

In fact, finding the right accountant, financial planner, estate planner, and other qualified experts is one of the most important decisions you will make in this process of becoming a resident.

CHAPTER NINE

BUILDING A TEAM TO WIN

EVERY COACH OF a professional sports team wants to recruit the best players so they can create a winning team, but this isn't always easy. The same goes for putting together a winning team of experts to help you establish residency in Florida. There are plenty of investment firms, advisors, and experts who will gladly manage your money and offer you advice, but each of them is going to provide a very different experience.

Financial experts operate within different models, specialize in different industries and areas, and offer different kinds of expertise. They might work at a local bank branch, a traditional investment firm, a full-service broker (often called a "wirehouse"), or an independent practice that has a major firm as its custodian. They may cater to specific client groups and provide varying levels of service and advice in money management. How in the world can you possibly figure out which financial advisor (or for that matter, accountant, insurance advisor, and estate planner) is right for you?

If you met with ten different financial advisors over the next week, you would probably get ten different recommendations for your financial plan and investment portfolio. To complicate the issue, you may already have a financial advisor, an accountant, an estate planning attorney, and other experts that you've worked with in a northern state somewhere. Maybe it took you a long time to find them, and you've established strong relationships over the years. Do you really have to find a whole new team just because you're becoming a Florida resident?

Our answer is, "Yes, you should probably think about putting together a Florida-based team." Why? Because experts who live and work in Florida are far more likely to understand the full implications of your change in residency as it affects your estate, finances, and investments. Of course, it's a not a requirement to work with a Florida financial advisor as a Florida resident, but it does further your intent and gravity to become a Florida resident when you work with trusted, local professionals—naturally, something most long-term residents of a state would be doing.

You want to find people you can fully trust and feel comfortable with, who are competent and possess plenty of knowledge and expertise to provide you with financial confidence. First of all, we recommend finding people who have experience working with clients who have made the transition from a northern state to Florida.

WHAT IS A FIDUCIARY, AND WHY IS THAT IMPORTANT?

Then, we recommend finding advisors who are held to a fiduciary standard of care. The world of investment advice evolves constantly due to changing regulations and technological advances, so it's important to have a financial advisor that is on your side. A fiduciary means that, when acting as an investment advisor representative, they are held to a fiduciary standard of care. That means they're required by law to only give you advice that's in your best interest.

How can you tell if someone is held to a fiduciary standard? Generally, if they're managing your accounts for a fee (rather than taking commissions off investments and financial products) and they're registered as an investment advisor representative, then they are being held to a fiduciary standard for those accounts. It's always a good idea to have a discussion with the financial advisor to get clarity on which accounts they're being held to a fiduciary standard of care.

Be aware, there are a wide variety of credentials that advisors can earn that give them the appearance of credibility, so do your research. Some credentials take several years of rigorous study and testing, as well as a lot of industry experience, to earn, while others simply take a few hours.

In our opinion, the gold standard in the investment industry is the Chartered Financial Analyst® designation, which is administered by the CFA Institute.[30] To earn the right to use the Chartered Financial Analyst® designation, an individual must undergo years of study and examination,

---

30 https://www.cfainstitute.org/en/about/governance/policies/trademark-usage-guide-for-cfa-charterholders.

using a curriculum that provides a deep understanding of the financial markets, and gain several years of industry experience.

Additionally, there's the CERTIFIED FINANCIAL PLANNER™ certification, which is administered by the Certified Financial Planner Board of Standards.[31] CFP® professionals are also held to high ethical standards and receive education about financial planning beyond simply investing.

So, if you're looking for a financial advisor in Florida that you can really trust, we recommend that you start by looking for three things:

- They're held to a fiduciary standard of care.
- They're a CFA® charterholder.
- They're a CFP® professional.

TAKING YOUR FIRST STEPS

When you finally decide that you want to start the process of becoming a Florida resident, you need a team that can put together a comprehensive financial plan that is customized to your situation. We recommend having your team conduct a quantitative analysis first to make sure the numbers work for you. Explore the impact of the Florida homestead exemption, estate taxes, the lack of state income taxes, and other factors on your financial plans so you can know what the actual monetary advantages are going to be.

Then, ask them to guide you through a qualitative analysis

---

31   https://www.cfp.net/career-and-growth/market-yourself/how-to-use-the-cfp-marks.

so you have a clear sense of the personal, emotional impact of making the move. Just because the numbers work in your favor doesn't mean the move is right for you and your family. There are plenty of personal considerations that you need to take into account as well.

As your team revisits and revises all of your financial documents, look for gaps, areas where you could save or invest more, documents that need to be updated to your new residence, and so on. Once all of your finances are in order, have a plan in place for your team to regularly monitor your plan to make sure everything stays current, up to date, and optimized.

With the right team, you can maximize the benefits of making Florida your new home, minimize any negatives, and set yourself up for greater success in the long run.

CHAPTER TEN

LIVING AND THRIVING IN FLORIDA

WHERE TO LIVE AND WHAT TO DO

You probably have some idea of what it's like to live in Florida based on things you have seen, heard, or read about—or given that you've already been living here part-time or on vacation over the years. As a mental exercise, think of five things that come to mind when you imagine what it's like to live here. Now, say them out loud. Go ahead.

Chances are, you said something about the weather (hurricanes, heat, and humidity), something about the laissez-faire attitude, maybe something about life on the beach, crazy drivers, and a certain quirky sensibility ("Florida Man," anyone?). Whatever the case, we're here to tell you that Florida is not just one culture, one temperament, one climate, or one way of life. Actually, the state is diverse enough that almost anyone can find a place to live here that matches their personality and preferences.

Do you prefer to live on the beach? Do you want to live in

a big bustling tourist town full of theme parks? Do you want to live in a high-energy party town full of different ethnic groups? Do you want to live in a quiet, backwoods town? Do you want to live in the Deep South, full of Southern charm and thick accents? Do you want to enjoy island living and spend all day on your boat?

You can have all of this and more. It just depends on where you decide to settle when you move to Florida. At the risk of generalizing too much, we would say that in our experience, if you want a place that's a little sleepy and laid-back, head to the West Coast of Florida. If you prefer a more fast-paced way of life, head to the East Coast. If you want island living, go to the Keys. If you want a big international city with a ton of family attractions, Orlando might be more your style.

If you want a party town with a lot of nightlife, Fort Lauderdale and Miami are full of energy. But if you want to live in the Deep South, then head to the panhandle. In fact, they say in Florida, "The farther north you go, the more Southern you get."

Maybe you love the outdoors. In that case, Florida has eleven national parks, the most famous of which is perhaps Everglades National Park, which stretches all the way from the Atlantic to the Gulf across the southern end of the Florida peninsula. This is your place to see alligators and crocodiles, dolphins, and all kinds of wading birds. There's also Biscayne National Park, which is 95 percent underwater. A great place for boating, scuba diving, and snorkeling.

There's the Timucuan Ecological Preserve near Jacksonville, which contains 46,000 acres of marshes, dunes, and hardwood trees, and is home to numerous historical sites. Or you can visit some of the nicest beaches in the country at Gulf Islands National Seashore.

SOME INTERESTING PLACES TO LIVE IN FLORIDA

Naples. A cozy town of just under 20,000 with a highly rated school system, Naples also has one of the highest percentages of millionaires of any city in the United States. Located in Southwest Florida, Naples is known for its abundant shopping, beautiful beaches, and amazing golf courses. It's also close to the Everglades.

Miami Beach. This coastal resort city of 77,000 people is known for its art deco architecture, amazing beaches, and exciting nightlife. It is definitely a party town, with a highly diverse population.

Sarasota. This Gulf Coast city offers a low cost of living, great beaches, and plenty of recreational activities. The real estate market is strong, the hospitals are highly rated, and there are plenty of outdoor festivals and events throughout the year.

Jacksonville. Located on the Atlantic coast in Northeast Florida, Jacksonville is the largest city by area in the entire country. With a population of over 962,000 people, it's also one of the most populous. Jacksonville's climate is a bit more temperate than other parts of the state, if that matters to you.

Key West. It takes a particular kind of person to really vibe with the island lifestyle of Key West. If you love a tropical climate, warm water, plenty of opportunities to fish, and a laid-back lifestyle, then this might be the place for you. Just remember, Key West is closer to Havana, Cuba, than to Miami. It's *way down there!*

CHAPTER TEN

Orlando. The theme park hub of Florida, this city draws millions of visitors from all over the world every year. A growing city of more than 300,000, it offers diverse culture, popular attractions, lower taxes, and a booming real estate market.[32]

The point is, you can find a place in Florida that fits your style, personality, and preferences (unless you just really want bitterly cold, snowy winters, in which case you might be out of luck).

CONFRONTING STEREOTYPES

There are plenty of stereotypes about Florida. As George Carlin said, "I like Florida. Everything is in the eighties. The temperatures, the ages, and the IQs." Of course, he was joking, but in our experience, this is simply not a fair representation of Florida as it is today.

Now, to be fair, *some* of the things you've heard about Florida are true. The state is about as flat as can be. Golf course hills are actually some of the higher points of elevation in the state, and the highest point of elevation in Florida is Britton Hill, located way up in the panhandle just two miles from the Alabama border. At just 345 feet above sea level, it's the lowest highpoint in the United States, so if you crave mountains, you might be out of luck in Florida!

Additionally, Florida *is* relatively warm, and you're going

---

32 "Cities in Florida by Population (2023)," World Population Review, 2023, https://worldpopulationreview.com/states/cities/florida.

to notice the difference if you come from a far northern state. It won't be all that different if you come from Georgia or Texas, but if you're used to the lake effect snow in Buffalo, it's going to be a noticeable change. Either you'll like it, or it will take adjusting to.

At the same time, the Florida heat is sometimes exaggerated. Across the state, summers average between 73 and 95 degrees, and if you're wary of the heat, there are some parts of the state that are a bit cooler. Florida's Historic Coast, which includes the cities of St. Augustine and Ponte Vedra, is a few degrees cooler than the rest of the state. Where we live, Naples, the hottest temperature on record is 99 degrees, so it has never reached 100 here (thank the Lord for the sea breeze).

At the same time, however, Florida humidity can be intense. There's no getting around it. Florida is without question the most humid state in the US.[33] Seventy-five percent of the land is on the coast, so the air is almost always moving over warm water and picking up water vapor.

There are some ways to deal with the humidity, though. Drink plenty of cool water. Go swimming or take a cool shower. Dress comfortably in loose, light clothing. Use a dehumidifier in your house. If the humidity is really a problem for you, then you can live in far north Florida or the panhandle, where it's much less humid and gets a little cooler in the winter. The "coldest" cities in Florida are Jasper, Crestview, Monticello, and Niceville, which are all in the north.[34]

---

[33] "Humidity in Florida," Florida Climate Center, accessed April 6, 2023, https://climatecenter.fsu.edu/topics/humidity.
[34] Pete Ortiz, "What Is the Coldest City in Florida? 2023 Update," House Grail, February 27, 2023, https://housegrail.com/coldest-city-in-florida.

CHAPTER TEN

What about the stereotype that says Florida is mostly a retirement community? Well, first of all, there *are* quite a few retirement communities across the state, but that doesn't mean it's a sleepy state full of tired retirees. On the contrary, Florida communities tend to be very active. With so many sunny days, there are always outdoor activities going on. Golf, tennis, pickleball, and fishing are nearly everywhere!

Also, as we said, Florida's not just one culture. It's not just retirement homes. You've got big urban cities like Miami, Jacksonville, Tampa, and Orlando. You've got tiny rural towns. You have cities that are very ethnically diverse. Basically, Florida has almost everything to offer. We love the culture, the climate, the people, the cities, and all of the activities that are available every day around the year, and we're convinced that there's a place for you here!

As we like to say, we live where other people vacation!

CONCLUSION

SUNSHINE STATE SUMMARY

WE TRIED TO set the stage at the very beginning of this book. If you're thinking about moving to Florida, there are a lot of things to consider. It's not as simple as it might seem! While the actual paperwork to become a Florida resident can essentially be completed in an afternoon, there's a lot more that you need to do, especially if you want to ensure a smooth transition to Florida from your former state. Our Sunshine State Strategy is designed to help you make the move in the right way, so you avoid potential headaches, overcome challenges, and make the most of the potential benefits.

After the dust has settled, we want you to have peace of mind that you moved to Florida for the right reasons and that you did it above board, so you can rest easy knowing that this is now your home.

First, we recommend conducting a quantitative analysis to make sure the numbers work for you. Work with a team of qualified experts to figure out exactly how you might benefit from becoming a Florida resident. How will the lack of state income tax, estate tax, and inheritance tax help keep more of your hard-earned wealth within your family? What about the business-friendly climate, the strong creditor protections, and the effects of the homestead exemption (and the termination of the one up north)?

Our goal on the quantitative side is to provide you with the data and information to ensure a move to Florida makes sense financially, given your situation. If the numbers work for you, then you should reflect from a qualitative perspective as well to ensure that the move will be a good thing for you and your family from a personal, emotional perspective. Will you be moving far away from loved ones? Will you struggle to leave a state that you know and love? Only you can determine if the financial benefits outweigh the personal cost.

We recommend bringing together a team of experts who are located in Florida, highly qualified people who can create a winning team to help you get all of your finances in order for the move. Members of your team should include an estate planning attorney, accountant, financial advisor, insurance advisor, and others. Go through all of your financial documents, make appropriate revisions, and update your information.

Are there gaps in your insurance coverage that need to be filled? Are there potential investment portfolio adjustments to consider once you've formalized your Florida residency? Will your investments and retirement accounts meet your long-term income goals? Is your estate plan in order, so your assets can pass to your heirs and beneficiaries smoothly and efficiently?

When you're ready to become a Florida resident, it's time to complete The Fundamental Five. First, spend time and build your time in Florida, so you can get comfortable with it. Then, it's time to visit your local government center to fill out a Declaration of Domicile, register your vehicle(s), get a Florida driver's license, and register to vote. Once The Fundamental Five are done, congratulations, you're well on your way to becoming a Florida resident! Thereafter, continue to weigh your other indicators of intent to move your residence to Florida from your northern state.

REMEMBER, WE'RE HERE TO HELP

If the idea of conducting a quantitative and qualitative analysis; of going through all of your financial documents, insurance documents, and investment portfolio; and of finding a place to live that meets your personality and preferences—if all of this seems overwhelming to you, then remember, we're here to help! You don't have to bear the burden all by yourself.

If you want more information, additional resources, or links to key websites about Florida residency, head to our website at www.SunshineStateStrategy.com. We want to help you make this decision from a position of clarity, with clear goals and a well-defined process, so you feel confident at the end of the day that you've completed the journey to becoming a Floridian both gracefully and successfully.

You can also reach out to us directly. We're ready to walk with you through the Sunshine State Strategy, so you can become a Florida resident and enjoy the life, culture, weather, activities, and financial benefits of living in the Sunshine State.

APPENDIX

ADDITIONAL RESOURCES

WE'VE PUT TOGETHER a list of resources to help you think through your move, including some sample documents from counties across the state.

THE OFFICIAL PAGE FOR THE STATE OF FLORIDA

https://www.myflorida.com/

Declaration of Domicile

Note: Some counties do not provide online Declaration of Domicile forms. In these instances, the form must be acquired in person or via mail from the county clerk.

* Denotes counties that we were able to easily locate the Declaration of Domicile form on the county clerk website.

You should also reach out to the county in which you

intend to move to ensure the most accurate and up-to-date information specific to that county is available.

- Alachua County*
- Baker County
- Bay County*
- Bradford County
- Brevard County*
- Broward County*
- Calhoun County
- Charlotte County*
- Citrus County*
- Clay County*
- Collier County*
- Columbia County
- DeSoto County
- Dixie County
- Duval County*
- Escambia County*
- Flagler County*
- Franklin County*
- Gadsden County*
- Gilchrist County
- Glades County
- Gulf County*
- Hamilton County
- Hardee County
- Hendry County
- Hernando County*
- Highlands County
- Hillsborough County*
- Holmes County
- Indian River County*
- Jackson County
- Jefferson County
- Lafayette County
- Lake County*
- Lee County*
- Leon County
- Levy County
- Liberty County
- Madison County
- Manatee County*
- Marion County*
- Martin County
- Miami-Dade County*
- Monroe County
- Nassau County*
- Okaloosa County*
- Okeechobee County
- Orange County*
- Osceola County*
- Palm Beach County*
- Pasco County*
- Pinellas County*
- Polk County
- Putnam County
- St. Johns County
- St. Lucie County*
- Santa Rosa County*
- Sarasota County*
- Seminole County*
- Sumter County*

APPENDIX

- Suwannee County*
- Taylor County
- Union County
- Volusia County*

- Wakulla County*
- Walton County*
- Washington County*

Links are being provided for information purposes only. Raymond James is not affiliated with and does not endorse, authorize, or sponsor any of the listed websites or their respective sponsors. Raymond James is not responsible for the content of any website or the collection or use of information regarding any website's users and/or members.

ABOUT THE AUTHORS

RYAN KINSER

Offering comprehensive and multigenerational financial planning, Ryan and the team specialize in tailored portfolio construction and a concierge level of client service.

"Our goal is for clients to feel as though they've found the perfect team to guide them throughout the remainder of their working years and retirement," Ryan said. "We want them to be confident in our plan for the future, learn along the way, and truly enjoy the experience in working with our team."

Ryan joined Raymond James Financial Services in May 2018, as a Financial Advisor where he co-founded his independent practice Oley Kinser Concierge Wealth, LLC, with his longtime friend and colleague from business school, Brett Oley. Previously, Ryan spent four years with Citigroup and five years with UBS Financial Services Inc.

"Brett and I are genuinely proud to be affiliated with Raymond James Financial Services, a firm where the culture truly aligns with our client-first focus, in addition to ethics and integrity being paramount," Ryan said. "Raymond James' commitment to innovation and technology is very impressive, while the firm also provides financial advisors with an ideal platform that allows their entrepreneurial spirit to flourish and create a positive client experience."

Ryan earned his Bachelor of Science in both economics and finance from the University of Central Florida and his

ABOUT THE AUTHORS

MBA from the University of Florida, and completed financial planning courses at Florida State University, which led him to become a CERTIFIED FINANCIAL PLANNER™ professional. Ryan has earned the right to use the Chartered Financial Analyst® designation and is also a member of the CFA® Society of Naples.

"I absolutely love finance and am a constant 'student of the game,'" Ryan said. "I've been blessed with the opportunity to combine my passion for finance with the ability to utilize the knowledge I have gained to help people reach for a lifetime of goals."

Ryan genuinely cares about more than just his clients' investment portfolios; he cares a great deal about who they are as people and their well-being. In doing business with Ryan, clients can expect a true concierge service experience including transparent advice, knowledge sharing and education, proactive communication, in-home meetings if preferred, and nearly 24/7 direct access, even on weekends.

"We firmly believe in doing what is right for the client at all times," said Ryan, who takes pride in his high ethical standard. "Clients will typically realize this early on in our professional relationship, as Brett and I are very genuine, straightforward, and fully transparent with them from the start."

Originally from Stuart, Florida, Ryan also spent five years on the Caribbean Island of St. Maarten. Ryan, his wife Dana, daughter Kaia, and two sons Barron and Troy reside in beautiful Naples, Florida.

When he is away from the office, he is an avid tennis player (4.0 level)—and enjoys playing golf, though he admits he has room for improvement.

ABOUT THE AUTHORS

BRETT OLEY

Brett Oley, a Co-Founder and Managing Partner of Oley Kinser Concierge Wealth and also a Financial Advisor of Raymond James Financial Services Inc., has built his advisory career on providing holistic wealth management—creating customized, comprehensive, and thoughtful plans and professional money management solutions. Trustworthy and knowledgeable, Brett's early fascination with finance, entrepreneurship, and stewardship has led him to build a team at Oley Kinser Concierge Wealth that works together to guide and educate families on ways to optimize their financial growth potential and preserve their wealth for the future. He specializes in helping business owners, retirees, families, and divorced individuals.

Delivering exceptional client service is second nature to Brett. He is ultra-passionate in his work and takes great pride in knowing all of his clients and understanding their unique needs. He makes every effort to provide friendly and impactful client interactions.

"Our mission is to build an innovative wealth management practice that not only continuously improves, but also helps provide value-creating solutions for our clients—all the while enjoying what we do," Brett said. "We thoughtfully work with each family to sincerely understand their needs and strive to make sure they are met with plans expertly customized to them."

Brett's advisory career began with UBS in 2006. He joined the independent contractor division of Raymond James in 2017.

"Raymond James allows us the independence to more successfully create a positive client experience and also take care of our team, so that we can reach our full potential," Brett said.

Brett graduated with a Bachelor's degree with a double major in Finance and Management (New and Small Business Concentration) from Georgetown University in 2004 and earned an MBA from the University of Florida at Gainesville in 2013.

An Accredited Wealth Management Advisor, Chartered Divorce Financial Analyst, Chartered Retirement Planning Counselor, and a CERTIFIED FINANCIAL PLANNER™ practitioner, Brett holds Series 7, 9, 10, 31, and 66 securities licenses and is also life, health, and variable annuity insurance licensed.

In 2020, Brett co-authored (with business partner Ryan Kinser) the book *Pillars of Planning: An Essential Guide to Help Grow and Protect Your Wealth*. The book covers an array of wealth management topics—providing value-added knowledge to the reader.

Brett hails from Vermilion, Ohio, a suburb of Cleveland situated on the south shore of Lake Erie. A Florida resident since 2006, Brett and his two beautiful children live in Naples with their French Bulldog "Atlas" and tabby cat "Oasa." Beyond time with family and friends, Brett enjoys exercising, reading, fishing, traveling, and always learning new things!

www.ingramcontent.com/pod-product-compliance
Lightning Source LLC
Chambersburg PA
CBHW070114080526
44586CB00013B/1295